ENGLISCH TRAINING

Paul Jenkinson
Englisch 5. Klasse
Grundlagen und
Aufgaben mit Lösungen

STARK

Dieser Band wurde nach der neuen Rechtschreibung abgefasst.

ISBN: 3-89449-320-8

© 1997 by Stark Verlagsgesellschaft mbH · D-85318 Freising · Postfach 1852 · Tel. (08161) 1790
1. Auflage 1997
Nachdruck verboten!

Inhalt

Vorwort an die Schüler
Vorwort an die Eltern

... rund ums Nomen

1	Plural	1
1.1	Pluralformen des Nomens	1
1.2	Mengenangaben mit *of*	5
2	Groß- und Kleinschreibung	9
3	Genitiv	15
3.1	*s*-Genitiv	15
3.2	*of*-Genitiv	18
4	Artikel	23
4.1	unbestimmter Artikel	23
4.2	bestimmter Artikel	26
5	Pronomen und Begleiter	29
5.1	Personalpronomen	30
5.3	Possessivbegleiter	38
5.4	Demonstrativpronomen und Demonstrativbegleiter	43
6	Ortsangaben	49
6.1	Präpositionen in Orts- und Richtungsangaben	49
6.2	Den Weg erklären	69
7	Zahlen, Datums- und Zeitangaben	75
7.1	Grundzahlen	75
7.2	Ordnungszahlen	77
7.3	Zeitangaben	80
7.4	Datum	84
7.5	Wochentage	87

Fortsetzung nächste Seite!

... rund ums Verb

| 8 | Adverbien der Zeit und Häufigkeit | 89 |

9	Zeitformen des Verbs	97
9.1	*simple present*	97
9.2	*present progressive*	109
9.3	*simple past*	118
9.4	*going-to-future*	125

10	Hilfsverben	131
10.1	*to be*	131
10.2	*have/has got*	136
10.3	Die modalen Hilfsverben *can*, *must* und *have*	143

... rund um den Satz

11	Gerundium als Subjekt	155
12	Imperativ	159
13	Fragen mit Fragewörtern	163
14	*there is-*, *there are*-Konstruktionen	179

Anhang

15	Homophone	181
16	Schwierige Wörter, die wir in diesem Buch benutzen	189
16.1	Englisch – Deutsch	189
16.2	Deutsch – Englisch	197

Lösungen zu den Übungsaufgaben 205

Autor und Illustrator: Paul Jenkinson

Vorwort an die Schülerinnen und Schüler

Liebe Schülerin, lieber Schüler,

dies ist das erste Jahr, in dem du Englisch lernst. Wie ist es dir bis jetzt ergangen? Macht dir das Englischlernen Spaß? Wie kommst du mit dem Vokabellernen zurecht? Es ist nicht leicht, eine neue Sprache zu lernen. Englisch ist aber ungemein wichtig, weil es eine Sprache ist, die du später oft gebrauchen wirst und mit der du dich fast überall auf der Welt verständigen kannst.

Dieses Buch hilft dir dabei mit **Erklärungen, Beispielen und zusätzlichen Übungen.** Alle wichtigen Regeln, die du im Englischunterricht der 5. Klasse kennen lernst, sind hier behandelt. Jedes Kapitel beginnt mit einer leicht verständlichen Erklärung und einem Beispielsatz dazu. Daran schließen sich langsam schwerer werdende Übungen an. Diese Übungen bauen häufig auf Bildern auf, um es für dich abwechslungsreicher zu machen. Damit du den Schwierigkeitsgrad der Übungen besser einschätzen kannst, haben wir die besonders schweren Übungen mit einem ✽ markiert. Selbstverständlich gibt es zu allen Übungen auch **Lösungen.**

Am Ende des Buches findest du ein **Vokabelverzeichnis,** das dir diejenigen Wörter erklärt, die du nicht kennst oder die du vergessen hast. Du kannst mit diesem Verzeichnis aber auch deinen Wortschatz erweitern.

Du musst dieses Buch nicht von der ersten bis zur letzten Seite durcharbeiten, sondern du solltest die Kapitel aussuchen, die für dich jeweils wichtig sind. Somit lässt sich das Buch auf vielfältige Weise benutzen: Du kannst

- immer an dem Kapitel arbeiten, das ihr gerade im Unterricht behandelt,
- zusätzlich für Klassenarbeiten bzw. Schulaufgaben üben,
- den Unterrichtsstoff wiederholen, den du bis jetzt gelernt hast,
- die Kapitel durcharbeiten, mit denen du Probleme hast.

Falls du einen Grammatikteil nicht verstehst, dann bitte deine Eltern oder deine Englischlehrerin bzw. deinen Englischlehrer um Hilfe.

Ich hoffe, dass dir die Übungen, Zeichnungen und Erklärungen, die ich für dich gemacht habe, Spaß machen und dass du aus ihnen viel lernen kannst.

Paul Jenkinson

Vorwort an die Eltern

Liebe Eltern,

dies ist das erste Jahr, in dem Ihr Kind Englisch lernt, und deshalb ist es ein besonders wichtiges Jahr. Denn nur wenn es den Englischstoff der 5. Klasse vollkommen verstanden hat und seine Anwendung beherrscht, wird das weitere Englischlernen problemlos sein. Dieses Buch kann Ihrem Kind in vielfältiger Weise helfen, eine gute Grundlage in Englisch zu bekommen.

- Der **gesamte Lernstoff der 5. Klasse** ist leicht verständlich erklärt und anhand von **Beispielen** verdeutlicht. Der Inhalt jedes Kapitels wird dann in einer Vielzahl von abwechslungsreichen **Übungen** trainiert.
- Die Übungen beginnen auf einem sehr einfachen Sprachniveau und werden dann schwieriger. Die vielen **Bilder** sollen den Lernprozess fördern und zum Spaß am Lernen beitragen.
- Ihr Kind sollte die Antworten erst dann mit den **Lösungen** am Ende des Buches vergleichen, wenn es sie schriftlich fixiert hat. Kennzeichnen Sie alles, was Ihrem Kind schwer fällt. Sie wissen dann, wo seine Schwächen liegen und worauf Sie bei der Wiederholung besonders achten müssen.
- Nicht nur das Erlernen der Sprachstruktur ist für Ihr Kind wichtig, sondern auch die Erweiterung seines **Wortschatzes** in der Fremdsprache. Natürlich wird es in diesem Buch Wörter geben, die Ihr Kind noch nicht kennt, deshalb steht am Schluss des Buches ein umfassendes Vokabelverzeichnis.

Ich hoffe, dass der spielerische Umgang mit der englischen Sprache, den ich in diesem Buch vermitteln möchte, ihr Kind beim anfangs so schwierigen Fremdsprachenerwerb erfolgreich unterstützt.

Paul Jenkinson

1 Plural

Du verwendest den **Singular,** also die Einzahl, wenn du ausdrücken möchtest, dass ein Wesen oder eine Sache nur **einmal** vorhanden ist.
Beispiel: I am eating an app<u>le</u>.
Ich esse einen <u>Apfel</u>.

Dagegen benutzt du den **Plural,** d. h. die Mehrzahl, wenn du von **mehreren** – mindestens aber von zwei – Wesen oder Dingen sprichst.
Beispiel: I am playing with my <u>friends</u>.
Ich spiele mit meinen <u>Freunden</u>.

1.1 Pluralformen des Nomens

Wann verwendest du Pluralformen des Nomens?
Du verwendest Pluralformen des Nomens, wenn du von **zwei oder mehr Dingen oder Wesen** sprechen möchtest.

Wie bildest du die Pluralformen von Nomen?
- Im Englischen musst du bei den meisten Nomen ein **-s an die Singularform** des Nomens hängen.
  Beispiel: dog ⟶ dog<u>s</u>
- An Nomen, die im Singular auf *-s, -ss, -ch, -sh* oder *-x* enden, musst du **-es** anhängen.
  Beispiel: gla<u>ss</u> ⟶ glass<u>es</u>

1

... rund ums Nomen: Plural

- Bei Nomen, die mit einem **Konsonanten + -y** enden, wird das *-y* zu *-ie + -s*.

  Beispiel: famil**y** ⟶ famil**ies**

- **Aber** wenn das Nomen auf einen **Vokal + -y** endet, verändert sich das *-y* nicht und du hängst einfach noch ein *-s* an.

  Beispiel: b**oy** ⟶ b**oys**

- Es gibt auch einige **unregelmäßige Pluralformen.** Diese musst du auswendig lernen.

  Beispiele: child ⟶ child**ren**

  man ⟶ m**e**n

  woman ⟶ wom**e**n

  scarf ⟶ scar**ves**

  potato ⟶ potato**es**

1. Sieh dir die Bilder an und vervollständige dann die Liste mit den richtigen Singular- und Pluralformen.

... rund ums Nomen: Plural

Singular   **Plural**

a) _____   _____

b) _____   _____

c) _____   _____

d) _____   _____

e) _____   _____

f) _____   _____

g) _____   _____

h) _____   _____

i) _____   _____

j) _____   _____

Die regelmäßigen Pluralformen musst du folgendermaßen aussprechen:

- [S] nach stimmlosem Konsonant [f, p, k, t, θ]

  Beispiele: books, hats, socks

- [Z] nach Vokal oder stimmhaftem Konsonant [b, d, g, m, n, v]

  Beispiele: apples, teachers, legs

- [IZ] nach den Zischlauten [s, z, dʒ, ʃ, tʃ]

  Beispiele: boxes, glasses, villages

... rund ums Nomen: Plural

2. Welche Sachen kannst du im Haus von Mrs Evans entdecken, die öfter als einmal vorhanden sind?

a) _____ b) _____
c) _____ d) _____
e) _____ f) _____
g) _____ h) _____
i) _____ j) _____

3. Ordne deine Antworten aus Aufgabe 2 in die richtige Gruppe ein.

[S]	[Z]	[IZ]

... rund ums Nomen: Plural

1.2 Mengenangaben mit *of*

Wann verwendest du Mengenangaben mit *of*?
Begriffe wie *water, tea, bread* kannst du nicht zählen. Du darfst sie nicht in den Plural setzen.
Willst du aber dennoch ausdrücken, dass du von diesen nicht-zählbaren Begriffen genau ein oder aber mehrere meinst, musst du das mit bestimmten Wortgruppen und dem Wort *of* umschreiben.

Wie bildest du Mengenangaben mit *of*?
Du bildest Mengenangaben mit *of*, indem du vor den nicht-zählbaren Begriff die Fügungen *(a) bar of ..., (a) pair of ..., (a) bottle of ..., (a) tin of ..., (a) packet of ..., (a) box of ..., (a) bucket of ...* stellst.

Beispiele: a packet of tea
two pairs of jeans

Der Plural wird also von dem Nomen, das die Mengenangabe enthält, gebildet und nicht vom Gegenstand selbst.

Beispiele: two bottles of milk
three buckets of water

4. Schreibe zu jedem Bild eine passende Mengenangabe mit *of*. Bilde auch jeweils den Plural.
   (Fange beim Plural mit zwei an und zähle dann bei jedem neuen Beispiel eins dazu, so dass die nächte Mengenangabe drei ist und so weiter.)

   a) a _____   two _____
   of soup   _____ soup

... rund ums Nomen: Plural

b) _____   three _____
   _____   _____

c) _____   _____
   _____   _____

d) _____   _____
   _____   _____

e) _____   _____
   _____   _____

f) _____   _____
   _____   _____

... rund ums Nomen: Plural

5. Auf dem Hof der Westward Farm ist immer viel los. Erkläre, was jede Person hat.

a) George has got four _____

b) Barbara has got _____

c) Anne _____

d) Tom _____

e) Grandfather _____

f) Grandmother _____

6. Übersetze die folgenden Sätze.

a) Mary isst eine Packung Kekse.
_____

b) John kauft zwei Flaschen Milch.
_____

c) Mrs Sampson wäscht sechzehn Paar Hosen!
_____

2 Groß- und Kleinschreibung

Anders als im Deutschen schreibt man im Englischen fast alle Wörter klein. Es gibt nur wenige Fälle, in denen du Wörter mit einem Großbuchstaben beginnen musst.

Welche Wörter musst du im Englischen groß schreiben?

- Wörter am Anfang von Sätzen
  Beispiel: The tree is small.

- Eigennamen und *I* (1. Person Singular)
  Beispiele: Janet, Paul

- Ortsnamen
  Beispiele: London, Paris

- Ländernamen und Adjektive, die Länder bezeichnen
  Beispiele: English, America

- Straßennamen
  Beispiele: Long Road, High Street

- Wochentage
  Beispiele: Monday, Tuesday

- Monatsnamen
  Beispiele: January, February

- Titel von Büchern, Filmen etc.
  Beispiele: English Training, Jurassic Park

- einige Abkürzungen
  Beispiele: Mr, Mrs, Miss, Dr, Rd., St., Ave., OK

... rund ums Nomen: Groß- und Kleinschreibung

- Die Wörter *aunt* und *uncle* musst du nur dann groß schreiben, wenn du sie zusammen mit dem Namen der Person verwendest, ansonsten schreibst du sie klein.

  Beispiele: My aunt is old.   My Aunt Jane is old.

- Wenn du *mum* und *dad* anstelle des Namens einer Person verwenden möchtest, musst du diese Wörter groß schreiben. In allen anderen Fällen musst du sie klein schreiben.

  Beispiele: This is Dad's car.   Here is my dad.

- Den ersten Satz eines Briefes musst du ebenfalls groß schreiben.

  Beispiel: Dear Wendy,
  We are happy that ...

1. Die Reporter des Fernsehprogramms 'Outside' haben in Amerika eine Reportage gemacht. Annabella hat eine Nachricht an ihr Büro in England gefaxt. Kannst du die Nachricht noch einmal in vollständigen Sätzen schreiben? Verwende Großschreibung wo nötig und ersetze die Schrägstriche (/) durch Punkte.

```
please read this fax/
it is from elizabeth
and me in america/
we're waiting for a
plane to london with
tom mcdonald from
scotland/tom has got
photos of lucy and i
have got the video of
new york/see you
tomorrow (wednesday)/
annabella
```

... rund ums Nomen: Groß- und Kleinschreibung

2. Beantworte die Fragen zum Fax in vollständigen Sätzen.
   a) Who is the fax from? (Von wem ist das Fax?)
      _The fax is from_____ _and_____
   b) But, who writes the fax? (Aber wer schreibt das Fax?)
      _____
   c) Where are they? (Wo sind sie?)
      _____
   d) What are they doing? (Was tun sie dort?)
      _____
   e) Who are Annabella and Elizabeth with? (Mit wem sind Annabella und Elizabeth zusammen?)
      _____
   f) Where is he from? (Woher kommt er?)
      _____
   g) Has Lucy got the photographs? (Hat Lucy die Fotos?)
      _____
   h) Who is 'i' in the fax? (Wer ist im Fax mit 'i' gemeint?)
      _____
   i) What has Annabella got? (Was hat Annabella dabei?)
      _____
   j) What day is it? (Welcher Wochentag ist es?)
      _____

3. Sieh dir den Stadtplan von Bishop's Lynn genau an. Beantworte dann die Fragen in vollständigen Sätzen.

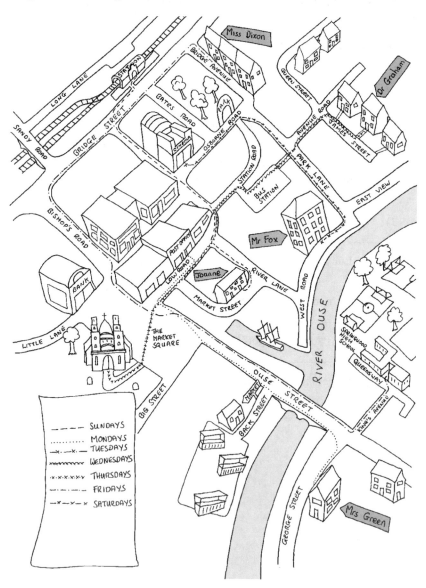

... rund ums Nomen: Groß- und Kleinschreibung

Wo wohnen Mr Fox, Mrs Green, Miss Dixon, Dr Graham und Joanne?
a) Mr Fox lives in _____
b) _____ lives in _____
c) _____
d) _____
e) _____

Wo befinden sich die folgenden Gebäude?
the cathedral, the cinema, the market, the post office, the train station, Springwood High School

f) The _____ is in _____
g) _____ is in _____
h) _____
i) _____
j) _____
k) _____

Wer tut was und an welchem Tag?
l) Mr _____ goes to _____ on _____
m) _____
n) _____
o) _____
p) _____

4. Wir haben einige neue Bücher herausgebracht und sie werden bald im Laden zu haben sein. Die Namen der Autoren geben versteckte Hinweise auf Monatsnamen. Das betreffende Buch kommt dann im darauffolgenden Monat zum Verkauf.

Kannst du die Bücher in der Reihenfolge ihres Erscheinens auflisten und den Erscheinungsmonat in Klammern schreiben? (Folge dem angegebenen Beispiel.) Wenn du für die Ordnungszahlen und die Monatsnamen Hilfe brauchst, dann schlage auf den Seiten 77 und 84 nach.

a) <u>The first book is The Clowns by Barry Fue*.</u> (March)

(*Barry Fue = February)

b) <u>The second book is Sea Birds by Lucy March.</u> (April)

c) The third book is _____ by _____ (____)

d) The fourth _____ (____)

e) The _____ (____)

f) _____ (____)

g) _____ (____)

h) _____ (____)

3 Genitiv

Der **Genitiv** ist der grammatische Fall, mit dem du einen **Besitz**, eine **Zugehörigkeit** oder eine **Bestimmung** ausdrücken kannst.

3.1 *s*-Genitiv

Wann verwendest du den *s*-Genitiv?
Du verwendest den *s*-Genitiv, um Besitz oder Zugehörigkeit anzuzeigen, wenn du von **Personen** oder **Tieren** sprichst.
Beispiele: It is <u>Mary's</u> book. Es ist Marys Buch.
This is the <u>dog's</u> mouth. Das ist die Schnauze des Hundes.

Wie bildest du den *s*-Genitiv?
Du bildest den *s*-**Genitiv im Singular**, indem du an die Singular-Form einen **Apostroph** und *s* anhängst.
Beispiel: Allan'<u>s</u> cat

... rund ums Nomen: Genitiv

1. Wem gehört was?

a) It's John's horse. _____ (John)
b) _____ (Peter)
c) _____ (Carol)
d) _____ (Arthur)
e) _____ (Amanda)
f) _____ (Jackie)
g) _____ (Kathy)

Bei **Pluralformen,** die **auf -s** enden, musst du nur einen **Apostroph** anhängen.

Beispiel: The boys' books.   (Die Bücher, die mehreren Jungen gehören.)

Bei **Pluralformen,** die **nicht auf -s** enden, musst du **Apostroph und s** anhängen, um den Genitiv Plural zu bezeichnen (wie beim Genitiv Singular).

Beispiel: The children's bedroom.
(Das Schlafzimmer, in dem mehrere Kinder schlafen.)

2. Vervollständige die folgenden Sätze. Die benötigten Wörter im Plural stehen in Klammern.

a) The _____ house. (sisters)

b) The _____ car. (policemen)

c) The _____ teacher. (children)

d) The _____ cat. (girls)

e) The _____ bus. (footballers)

f) It's the _____ photograph. (parents)

g) It's the _____ clothes shop. (women)

h) It's the _____ shoe shop. (men)

i) It's the _____ party. (boys)

3. Bei den gesperrt gedruckten Wörtern fehlen die Apostrophe. Kannst du sie ergänzen?

a) Today it's my brothers birthday, they are twins.

b) It's my grandfathers birthday.

c) Jackies car is green.

d) Roberts bedroom is small.

e) In Great Britain, a policemans uniform is black. Policewomens uniforms are also black.

f) The old car is grandmothers.

g) The girls are called Heather and Georgina. The girls uncle is called Henry.

h) The womens football team plays football on Fridays.

i) It's Margarets pen, the teachers chair, the boys pencils, and the girls books, but it's the schoolchildrens room.

j) The cats ear.

3.2 *of*-Genitiv

Wann verwendest du den *of*-Genitiv?
Du benutzt den *of*-Genitiv nur bei **Gegenständen.** Damit zeigtst du an, welcher Gegenstand zu einem anderen, meist größeren Gegenstand gehört.
Beispiele: the window of the house   das Fenster des Hauses

Wie bildest du den *of*-Genitiv?
Du bildest den *of*-Genitiv, indem du **vor das Nomen, das im Genitiv stehen soll, *of the* stellst.**
Beispiel: the handle of the door   der Griff der Tür

4. Schaue dir die folgenden Bilder an und schreibe dazu Ausdrücke, in denen du den *of*-Genitiv benutzt.

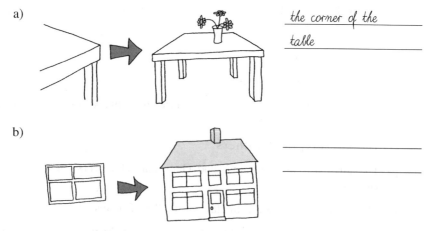

a) the corner of the table

b) _____

... rund ums Nomen: Genitiv

c)

d)

e)

f)

g)

... rund ums Nomen: Genitiv

5. Kannst du zu jeder Zeichnung einen Ausdruck mit einem *of*-Genitiv finden? Für die Wörter, die du dazu brauchst, habe ich einige Hinweise besonders deutlich gezeichnet.

a)

b)

c)

d)

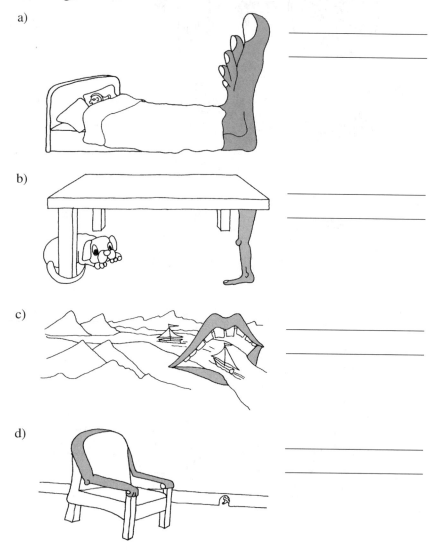

... rund ums Nomen: Genitiv

6. **Gemischte Übung:** Vervollständige die folgenden Sätze mit den richtigen Genitivformen (*'s / s' / of*).

   a) The _____ is big. (girl / bag)

   b) The _____ is green. (door / shop)

   c) The _____ is in the kitchen. (cat / milk)

   d) Jane has got a _____. (map / Scotland)

   e) The _____ is called Mr Williams. (children / teacher)

   f) The _____ is very good. (pop group / new CD)

   g) It's a _____. (man / hand)

   h) The accident is in the _____. (middle / road)

   i) The _____ plays on Saturdays. (women / basketball team)

   j) It's _____. (Jack / book)

   k) The _____ is Mrs Hope. (boys / mother)

   l) The _____ is white. (colour / door)

7. Übersetze die folgenden Sätze.

   a) Carols Hund ist groß.

   _____

   _____

   b) Die Tür des Hauses ist rot.

   _____

   _____

   c) Die Schule der Kinder ist in Newcastle-upon-Tyne.

   _____

   _____

   d) Die Schwester der Brüder heißt Mary.

   _____

   _____

4 Artikel

Nomen werden häufig zusammen mit einem Begleiter gebraucht. Einer dieser Begleiter ist der Artikel. Sowohl den bestimmten Artikel *(the)* als auch den unbestimmten *(a, an)* kannst du in den meisten Fällen genauso benutzen wie im Deutschen.

4.1 unbestimmter Artikel

Wann verwendest du den unbestimmten Artikel?
Du verwendest den **unbestimmten Artikel** vor einem Nomen, wenn du von einer **nicht näher bestimmten Person oder Sache** sprichst.
Beispiel: a dog   ein Hund (also irgendein Hund und nicht ein ganz bestimmter)

Wie verwendest du den unbestimmten Artikel bzw. wie sprichst du ihn aus?
Der unbestimmte Artikel *a* bzw. *an* wird für Nomen im Singular verwendet.
- **Vor einem Konsonanten** wird der unbestimmte Artikel *a* verwendet und [ə] ausgesprochen.
  Beispiel: a bus
- **Vor einem Vokal** wird der unbestimmte Artikel *an* verwendet und [ən] ausgesprochen. Vor einem Wort mit einem *u* am Anfang, das [ju] gesprochen wird (z. B. *uniform*) wird der unbestimmte Artikel *a* benutzt.
  Beispiel: an eye

... rund ums Nomen: Artikel

1. Schreibe den passenden unbestimmten Artikel vor die folgenden Wörter.

a) _____ orange   b) _____ dog
c) _____ cat   d) _____ answer
e) _____ uniform   f) _____ pen
g) _____ school   h) _____ island
i) _____ clock   j) _____ egg

2. Peter Casso, ein berühmter moderner Künstler, hat gerade sein letztes Meisterwerk beendet. Kannst du alle zehn Gegenstände erkennen, die er gezeichnet hat, und sie mit dem richtigen unbestimmten Artikel versehen?

... rund ums Nomen: Artikel

Im Englischen verwendest du den unbestimmten Artikel *a* bzw. *an* auch, wenn du über **Berufe** sprichst. Im Deutschen benutzt du ihn in diesem Fall aber nicht.
Beispiel: He is a policeman.   Er ist Polizist.

3. Beschreibe, welchen Beruf die folgenden Leute haben.

a) _I am a shop assistant._

b) He _____

c) She _____

d) He _____

e) She _____

f) I _____

4. Übersetze die folgenden Sätze.

a) Sie ist Lehrerin.

_____

b) Es ist ein Apfel.

_____

c) Ein Haus, ein Regenschirm und eine Tür.

_____

4.2 bestimmter Artikel

Wann verwendest du den bestimmten Artikel?

Im Allgemeinen verwendest du den **bestimmten Artikel** vor einem Nomen, wenn du nicht von irgendeiner Person oder Sache sprichst, sondern von einer ganz bestimmten.

Beispiel: the dog   der Hund (also der ganz bestimmte Hund und nicht irgendeiner)

Wie verwendest du den bestimmten Artikel bzw. wie sprichst du ihn aus?

Der bestimmte Artikel *the* wird für Nomen sowohl im Singular als auch im Plural verwendet.

- **Vor einem Konsonanten** sprichst du den bestimmten Artikel [ðə] aus.

  Beispiel: the car

- **Vor einem Vokal** sprichst du ihn [ði] aus. Vor einem *u*, das [ju] gesprochen wird (z. B. *uniform*), wird der bestimmte Artikel [ðə] gesprochen.

  Beispiel: the apple

5. Schreibe, was du auf den folgenden Bildern siehst, und benutze den bestimmten Artikel.

a) _____ b) _____
c) _____ d) _____
e) _____ f) _____
g) _____ h) _____
i) _____ j) _____

6. Welche der bestimmten Artikel aus Aufgabe 5 werden [ðə] und welche [ði] gesprochen?

[ðə]   [ði]

5 Pronomen und Begleiter

Wenn du im Englischen – ebenso wie im Deutschen – ein Nomen in einem ganzen Satz benutzen willst, musst du ihm fast immer einen **Begleiter** voranstellen. Ausnahmen sind Eigennamen.

Beispiele: The / Her / This house is big.
Kevin is tall.

Wenn du einmal ein Nomen benutzt hast, brauchst du es direkt danach nicht noch einmal zu benutzen. Derjenige, mit dem du sprichst oder dem du schreibst, wird nicht sofort das Nomen, das du genannt hast, vergessen. Deshalb kannst du in solchen Fällen das **Nomen** durch ein **Pronomen** ersetzen.

Beispiel: Mrs O'Brian is my English teacher. Mrs O'Brian is from Ireland.
Mrs O'Brian is my English teacher. She is from Ireland.

5.1 Personalpronomen

Das Personalpronomen (persönliches Fürwort) steht stellvertretend für eine Person oder Sache.

Rund um das Personalpronomen als Subjekt des Satzes

Wann verwendest du die Subjektform des Personalpronomens?
Du verwendest die **Subjektform des Personalpronomens**, wenn du in einem Satz ein Nomen ersetzen möchtest, das **Subjekt des Satzes** ist.
Beispiel: Susan and Tom live in Belfast.   They live in Belfast.

Im Englischen verwendest du im Singular bei **Personen** nur *he* oder *she*, für alles andere musst du *it* benutzen, mit Ausnahme von Tieren, deren Namen du kennst. In diesem Fall gebrauchst du ebenfalls *he* oder *she*.
Beispiele: It is a big horse.
Ned is a big horse. He is black and white.

Welche Subjektformen des Personalpronomens gibt es?

Kasus	Subjektform
1. Person, Singular	I
2. Person, Singular	you
3. Person, Singular	he, she, it
1. Person, Plural	we
2. Person, Plural	you
3. Person, Plural	they

Diese Formen musst du unbedingt **auswendig lernen** und immer wieder einmal wiederholen.

1. Ersetze in den folgenden Sätzen das Subjekt durch die entsprechenden Personalpronomen.

   a) Mike rides a horse.
      He rides a horse.

   b) The dog is very large.

   c) Harold and Julie are brother and sister.

   d) Jenny and I are cousins.

   e) The bus is from Aberdeen.

   f) Maggie is an old cat.

   g) Lucy, Martin, Ann and Peter go to school together.

   h) The birds wake Karen up in the morning.

   i) Judith plays golf.

   j) Tony, Tanya and I are good friends.

   k) The house is small.

   l) Mr Andrews is a taxi driver.

   m) John and Kathy live in Wales.

   n) Emma reads comics.

2. Ergänze die fehlenden Personalpronomen.

3. Auf wen beziehen sich die unterstrichenen Personalpronomen? Schreibe sie in der vorgegebenen Reihenfolge.

a) I = _____   b) he = _____

c) she = _____   d) I = _____

Schreibe das passende Personalpronomen für jede der folgenden Kombinationen auf.

e) Callum _____   f) Wendy and Callum _____

g) Nibbles _____   h) a mouse _____

i) Callum and I _____

Schreibe deine Antworten zusammen mit denen von a, b, c und d in die Wolkenkratzer.

✱ 4. Übung zum Wortschatz und zum Alphabet: Wo wohnen Wendy und Callum? Die dick umrandeten Quadrate in den Wolkenkratzern nennen dir den Namen einer englischen Stadt.

___ ___ ___ ___ ___ ___ ___ ___ ___

a) Wie viele Wörter kannst du aus den Buchstaben dieser Stadt bilden? Du darfst jeden Buchstaben nur einmal in jedem Wort verwenden.

b) Wie weit kannst du in einer Alphabetpyramide kommen? Verwende nacheinander die Buchstaben aus dem Namen der Stadt, um die Spitze einer Pyramide zu bilden. Es kann jeweils nur ein weiterer Buchstabe in jeder neuen Zeile der Pyramide verwendet werden. Jede Zeile muss ein englisches Wort ergeben. (Achtung: Nicht jeder Buchstabe der Stadt kann für die Spitze einer Pyramide verwendet werden.)

Beispiel:

... rund ums Nomen: Pronomen und Begleiter

Rund um das Personalpronomen als Objekt des Satzes

Wann verwendest du die Objektform des Personalpronomens?
Du verwendest die **Objektform des Personalpronomens,** wenn du in einem Satz ein Nomen ersetzen möchtest, das **Objekt des Satzes** ist.
Beispiel: I can see Peter.   I can see him.

Im Englischen gibt es keinen Unterschied zwischen den Formen für den Dativ und den Akkusativ, d. h. die Formen sind gleich.

Welche Objektformen des Personalpronomens gibt es?

Kasus	Objektform
1. Person, Singular	me
2. Person, Singular	you
3. Person, Singular	him, her, it
1. Person, Plural	us
2. Person, Plural	you
3. Person, Plural	them

Diese Formen musst du ebenfalls **auswendig lernen** und immer wieder einmal wiederholen.

5. Ersetze in den folgenden Sätzen die unterstrichenen Wörter durch die entsprechenden Objektformen des Personalpronomens.

   a) We can visit John today.
      We can visit him today.

   b) Give Mary the newspaper, please.
      _____

   c) Can you take Kim and me to the pop concert?
      _____

   d) I have a good name for the new song.
      _____

... rund ums Nomen: Pronomen und Begleiter

e) Carol buys <u>Jacob</u> a new coat.

f) I can see <u>Uncle George and Aunty Margaret</u> tomorrow.

g) Teacher: "I want <u>the class</u> to watch Robin Hood."

6. Vervollständige den Dialog, indem du die passenden Personalpronomen einsetzt.

– Hello, is that Gill?
– Yes, it is. Oh, hello Karen.
– Gill, can you help _____? I must talk to Ian.
– No problem, I can get _____ for you.
– Hello, Karen.
– Hello, Ian. Ian, Geoffrey and Janet's car has got a flat tyre (*platter Reifen*), can you drive _____ to the airport tonight?
– Karen, I'm sorry I can't drive _____. Jack lives near the airport, I can ask _____.
– Thanks Ian.
– Hello, Karen. Send _____ to Jack's office at 4.00 p.m. to meet _____. He can take _____ to the airport.
– Thank you again, Ian. Perhaps I can help _____ next time.

35

... rund ums Nomen: Pronomen und Begleiter

7. Setze die entsprechenden Personalpronomen der Objektform für die deutschen Pronomen ein.

a) mich _____   b) uns _____

c) euch _____   d) sie _____

e) ihnen _____   f) dir _____

g) ihn _____   h) mir _____

i) dich _____   j) ihm _____

k) Sie _____

8. Übersetze die folgenden Sätze.

a) Zoe hat einen Brief für dich.
_____

b) Ruth fährt uns zur Schule.
_____

c) Kannst du mich bitte anrufen?
_____

d) Vielleicht können sie uns besuchen.
_____

e) Er trifft sie (Singular) heute.
_____

f) Peter hat ein neues Auto. Er wäscht es gerade.
_____

g) Sie geht mit ihm ins Kino.
_____

h) Sharons Hund ist klein, kannst du ihn sehen?
_____

9. **Gemischte Übung:** Personalpronomen in der Subjekt- und Objektform.
In Aufgabe 6 hat Karen das Problem, dass Geoffrey und Janet zum Flughafen gebracht werden müssen. Hier sind einige Sätze über ihr Telefongespräch. Kannst du die Namen durch die passenden Personalpronomen in der Subjekt- und Objektform ersetzen?

a) First, Karen talks to Gill.
   First, she talks to her.

b) Karen asks Gill to help.
   _____

c) Karen talks to Ian.
   _____

d) Ian can't drive Geoffrey and Janet to the airport.
   _____

e) Ian asks Jack to help.
   _____

f) Jack can help Geoffrey and Janet.
   _____

g) Geoffrey and Janet meet Jack at 4.00 p.m.
   _____

h) Geoffrey and Janet go to the airport with Jack.
   _____

i) Karen thanks Ian.
   _____

5.2 Possessivbegleiter

Wann verwendest du Possessivbegleiter?
Du benutzt **Possessivbegleiter,** wenn du ein **Besitzverhältnis,** eine **Zugehörigkeit** oder eine **Verbundenheit** beschreiben möchtest.
Beispiele: M̲y bicycle is red.
That is ou̲r house.

Welche Possessivbegleiter gibt es?

Kasus	Possessivbegleiter
1. Person, Singular	my
2. Person, Singular	your
3. Person, Singular	his, her, its
1. Person, Plural	our
2. Person, Plural	your
3. Person, Plural	their

Diese Formen musst du unbedingt **auswendig lernen** und regelmäßig wiederholen.

Man kann leicht einige Possessivbegleiter mit anderen Wörtern verwechseln, z. B. *its/it's, their/there, your/you're.* Dieses Problem werden wir im Kapitel "Homophone" (gleichlautende Ausdrücke) ab Seite 181 behandeln.

10. Trudy sagt dir einiges über sich selbst. Kannst du vervollständigen, was sie sagt, indem du Possessivbegleiter einsetzt? Die Wörter, die du brauchst, stehen in der folgenden Liste, aber nicht in der richtigen Reihenfolge.
my, my, our, my, her, our, my, her, their, his, my

11. Auf dem Fundbüro: Ergänze die fehlenden Wörter.

a) "Have you got _____ umbrellas? _____ umbrella is black and white and _____ umbrella is black."

b) "They haven't got _____ coats."

c) "Are _____ coats long or short?"

d) "Long."

e) "Long, too, but _____ coat hasn't got _____ belt (*Gürtel*)."

f) "I haven't got _____ ball!"

g) "_____ friend hasn't got _____ shoe!"

... rund ums Nomen: Pronomen und Begleiter

12. Kannst du die Titel dieser Bücher übersetzen, die ich in einem deutschen Buchladen gefunden habe?

a) _____

b) _____ (Plural)

c) _____

d) _____

13. Gemischte Übung: Personalpronomen (in der Subjekt- und Objektform) und Possessivbegleiter.
Sieh dir die Bilder genau an, um herauszufinden, wer spricht und auch über wen die Sprecher reden. Dann vervollständige die Sätze.
Setze die Namen der Länder, aus denen die Personen kommen, in das Puzzle am Ende der Übung ein. Woher kommt die Person aus Bild h? Lies dafür die Buchstaben in den grau hinterlegten Quadraten von oben nach unten.

a)

_____ country is famous for _____ monster.

... rund ums Nomen: Pronomen und Begleiter

... rund ums Nomen: Pronomen und Begleiter

5.3 Demonstrativpronomen und Demonstrativbegleiter

Wann verwendest du Demonstrativpronomen und Begleiter?
Du verwendest **Demonstrativpronomen** (hinweisende Fürwörter) dann, wenn du auf etwas **ganz bestimmtes hinweisen** möchtest. Wenn du die Demonstrativpronomen vor einem Nomen verwendest, haben sie die Funktion von Demonstrativbegleitern. Wenn sie alleine stehen, sind sie Pronomen.
Beispiele: That bus is our school bus.
This is a car.

Welche Demonstrativpronomen gibt es?
this ⟶ Person und Ding in der **Nähe** des Sprechers
that ⟶ Person und Ding in einiger **Entfernung** vom Sprecher

14. Sieh dir die Zeichnungen genau an und erkläre, was sie zeigen. Schreibe dazu zwei Sätze.

a)
This is a cat.
That is a dog.

b)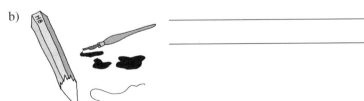

... rund ums Nomen: Pronomen und Begleiter

... rund ums Nomen: Pronomen und Begleiter

Willst du zwei Personen oder Sachen einander gegenüberstellen, verwendest du zuerst *this* und dann *that*.
Beispiel: <u>This</u> is Laura and <u>that</u> is Mike.

15. Vervollständige die folgenden Sätze anhand der Bilder.

a)    _____ is Tricia and _____ is Robin.

b)    _____ is a _____ book and _____ is a _____ book.

c)    _____ is a _____ and _____ is a _____ .

... rund ums Nomen: Pronomen und Begleiter

d) _____ is my _____ and _____ is my _____.

e) _____

f) _____

g) _____

... rund ums Nomen: Pronomen und Begleiter

these und *those* sind die Pluralformen von *this* und *that*.

Beispiele: This is a book.   These are books.
That is a letter.   Those are letters.

16. Hier sind zwei Pyramiden voller Gegenstände. Die linke ist in deiner Nähe und die rechte ist weiter weg. Verbinde die Gegenstände in sinnvoller Weise und schreibe dazu zwei Sätze.

a) These are tennis balls.   Those are footballs.

b) _____   _____

c) _____   _____

d) _____   _____

e) _____   _____

f) _____   _____

... rund ums Nomen: Pronomen und Begleiter

17. An Jasons Verkaufsstand auf dem Markt gibt es viele verschiedene Dinge. Was sagt er zu seinen Kunden?

a) _These are_ blue jeans and _those are_ black trousers.

b) _____

c) _____

d) _____

e) _____

f) _____

18. Gemischte Übung: Vervollständige die folgenden Sätze, indem du *this, that, these* und *those* zusammen mit einer Form von *to be* verwendest.

a) _This is_ a new house but _those are_ very old houses.

b) _____ _____ English newspapers. _____ _____ a German newspaper.

c) _____ _____ Adrian and _____ _____ Penny.

d) _____ _____ cats and _____ _____ dogs.

e) _____ _____ an American footballer and _____ _____ English footballers.

f) _____ _____ an apple but _____ _____ an orange, over there.

6 Ortsangaben

Manchmal ist es notwendig, anderen Menschen mitzuteilen, wo sich eine Person oder ein Gegenstand befindet. In diesen Fällen musst du in deiner Rede **Präpositionen** bzw. **feste Redewendungen** benutzen.

6.1 Präpositionen in Orts- und Richtungsangaben

Wann verwendest du Präpositionen in Orts- und Richtungsangaben?

Präpositionen sind **Verhältniswörter** wie z. B. *under, between, for*. Sie stehen meist vor einem Nomen oder einem Pronomen. Du verwendest Präpositionen in Orts- und Richtungsangaben, wenn du sagen möchtest, was wo ist, wohin sich etwas bewegt usw.

behind/ in front of

- *behind*
  Beispiel: The ball is behind the chair.

- *in front of*
  Beispiel: The apple is in front of the bottle.

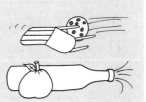

... rund ums Nomen: Ortsangaben

1. Lord und Lady Braybrook sind zu Hause in Braybrook Hall. Beschreibe, wo sich alles in Bezug auf Braybrook Hall befindet, indem du *behind* oder *in front of* benutzt.

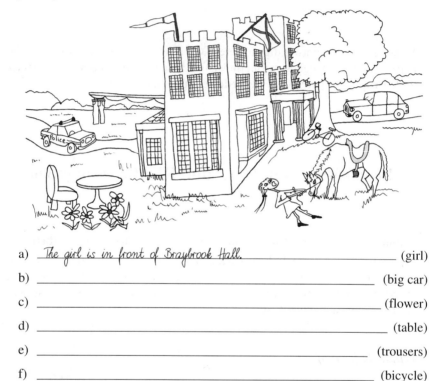

a) The girl is in front of Braybrook Hall. _____ (girl)
b) _____ (big car)
c) _____ (flower)
d) _____ (table)
e) _____ (trousers)
f) _____ (bicycle)
g) _____ (tree)
h) _____ (police car)
i) _____ (horse)

2. Übersetze die folgenden Sätze.

   a) Der Elefant ist hinter der Giraffe.

   b) Das Auto steht vor dem Supermarkt.

... rund ums Nomen: Ortsangaben

---

next to / next door to / near

- *next to*
  Beispiel: Kim is <u>next to</u> Colin.

- *next door to*
  Beispiel: Peter lives <u>next door to</u> Lucy.

- *near*
  Beispiel: Jenny is <u>near</u> the shop.

---

3. Bilde Sätze mit *near*, *next to* und *next door to*. Die Namen der Leute und die Verben, die du benötigst, stehen in Klammern. Aufgepasst: In zwei Sätzen darfst du nur das *simple present* verwenden, nicht die Verlaufsform!

a)    *Patricia is sitting next to the telephone.*
(Patricia / sit)

b)    _____
(Tom / stand)

c)    _____
(Carol / live)

... rund ums Nomen: Ortsangaben

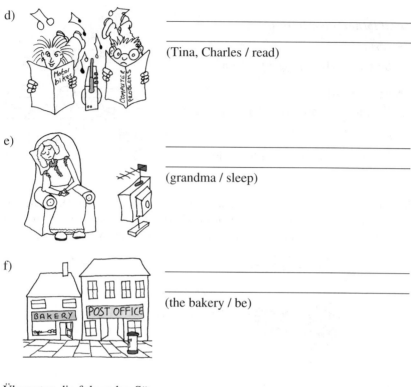

d) _____
(Tina, Charles / read)

e) _____
(grandma / sleep)

f) _____
(the bakery / be)

4. Übersetze die folgenden Sätze.

a) Der Ball ist neben dem Baum.

_____

b) Der Hund ist in der Nähe des Mädchens.

_____

c) Der Polizist wohnt neben dem Lehrer.

_____

... rund ums Nomen: Ortsangaben

outside/inside

- *outside*

    Beispiel: My car is <u>outside</u> my house.

- *inside*

    Beispiel: Paula is <u>inside</u> the bank.

5. Hier ist ein Bild von Tinas und Tims Spielzeugkiste. Erkläre, wo sich die Spielsachen jeweils befinden, indem du *inside* und *outside* verwendest.

... rund ums Nomen: Ortsangaben

a) *The bus is outside the toy box.* _____ (bus)
b) _____ (car)
c) _____ (elephant)
d) _____ (telephone)
e) _____ (plane)
f) _____ (shop)
g) _____ (house)
h) _____ (ball)
i) _____ (clown)
j) _____ (train)

6. Übersetze die folgenden Sätze und zeichne dann ein Bild zu deiner Antwort.

   a) Die Flaschen sind außerhalb der Häuser.
   _____

   b) Der Fernsehapparat ist im Geschäft.
   _____

   c) Roberts belegte Brote sind in seiner Tasche.
   _____

   a)   b)   c)

... rund ums Nomen: Ortsangaben

on top of / under

- *on top of*
  Beispiel: The shoes are <u>on top of</u> the chair.

- *under*
  Beispiel: The letter is <u>under</u> the book.

7. Beverlys Schreibtisch ist immer in Unordnung. Kannst du ihr helfen, die Dinge zu finden, die sie braucht?

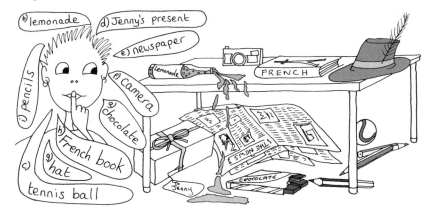

(desk = Schreibtisch)

a) *The chocolate is under the desk.*

b) _____

c) _____

d) _____

e) _____

f) _____

g) _____

h) _____

i) _____

... rund ums Nomen: Ortsangaben

> ***on the left / on the right / in the middle (of)***
>
> - *on the left*
>   Beispiel: My house is <u>on the left</u>.
>
> - *on the right*
>   Beispiel: The door is <u>on the right</u>.
>
> - *in the middle (of)*
>   Beispiele: My coat is <u>in the middle</u>.
>   The book shop is <u>in the middle of</u> the town.

8. Sieh dir die folgenden Bilder genau an und beschreibe, wo sich der Gegenstand oder die Person jeweils befindet.

a)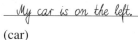
(car)

b)
(Mike)

56

... rund ums Nomen: Ortsangaben

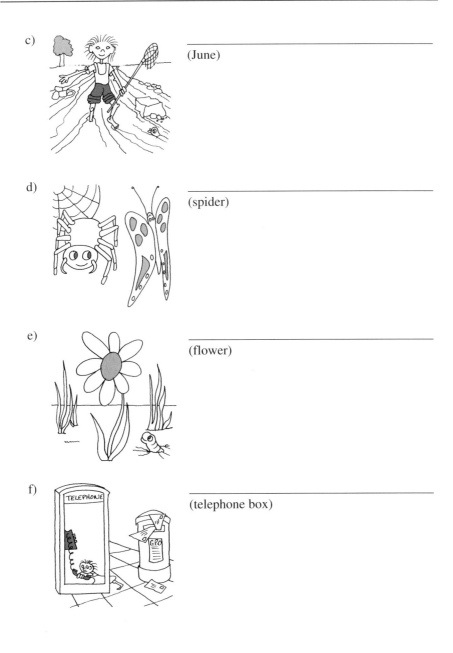

c) _____ (June)

d) _____ (spider)

e) _____ (flower)

f) _____ (telephone box)

... rund ums Nomen: Ortsangaben

9. Übersetze die folgenden Sätze.

   a) Johns Foto ist in der Mitte.

   b) Das Telefon ist auf der linken Seite.

   c) James ist auf der rechten Seite.

10. **Gemischte Übung:** Wie gut beherrschst du die bis jetzt gelernten Präpositionen? Kannst du aus den Informationen, die ich dir gebe, eine Zeichnung meines Arbeitszimmers anfertigen?
    Die Gegenstände, die du einzeichnen sollst, sind in der richtigen Größe dargestellt.

   - My desk is in the middle of the study.
   - My chair is behind my desk.
   - Behind my chair is one window.
   - The door is in front of my desk and it is in the middle of the wall.
   - My second window is in the middle of the wall to the right.
   - Under this window is my radiator.
   - My computer table is on the left next to my desk and on top of it is my computer.
   - Near my computer there is a wall with book shelves.
   - On top of my desk is my telephone.
   - Next to the door there is a painting and a plant. They are in front of my computer table. The plant is on the right and the painting is on the left.

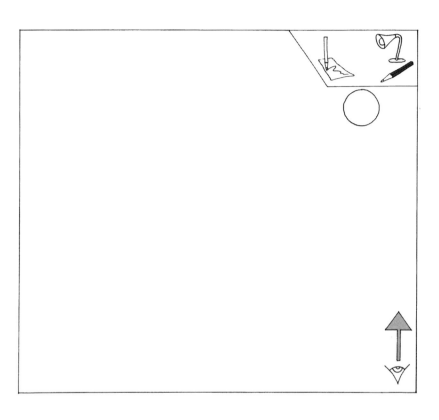

* **11.** Beantworte nun einige Fragen zu meinem Arbeitszimmer.

   a) Where is the door?

   b) Where is my computer?

   c) Where is my drawing table?

   d) Where is my stool?

   e) Where is the lamp?

... rund ums Nomen: Ortsangaben

at/across

- *at*

  Beispiel: He is waiting <u>at</u> the bus stop.

- *across*

  Beispiele: She walks <u>across</u> the road.

  The café is <u>across</u> the street.

12. Sieh dir die Zeichnungen sorgfältig an und vervollständige dann die Sätze, indem du *at* oder *across* einsetzt.

a)    Martha always meets Amy _____ the bookshop.

b)    Jack waits for Colin _____ the park.

c)    Tina sees Martin _____ the street.

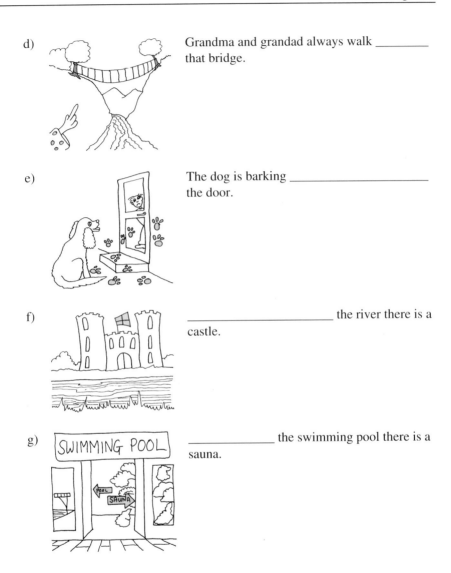

d) Grandma and grandad always walk _____ that bridge.

e) The dog is barking _____ the door.

f) _____ the river there is a castle.

g) _____ the swimming pool there is a sauna.

h) The food _____ school is good.

i) On Saturdays she rides her mountain bike _____ those mountains.

j) Pam must phone Tony _____ the station.

13. Übersetze die folgenden Sätze.

a) Die Post ist auf der anderen Straßenseite.

b) Paula trifft Ian am Bahnhof.

c) Carol darf nicht über den Rasen (= Gras) gehen.

in/into

- *in*
  Beispiel: The cat is <u>in</u> the garden.

- *into*
  Beispiel: Susan is putting the ball <u>into</u> the box.

14. Beschreibe die Szene, indem du *in* oder *into* verwendest. Namen und Schlüsselwörter stehen als Hilfe in Klammern.

a) _Amanda is in the café._ _____ (Amanda / café)

b) _____ (car / garage)

c) _____ (Peter / shop)

d) _____ (Mr and Mrs Little / car)

e) _____ (John's keys)

f) _____ (grandad / cassette / Walkman)

g) _____ (Mr Smith / post office)

h) _____ (Julia's camera)

i) _____ (robber / bank)

j) _____ (more robbers / bank)

... rund ums Nomen: Ortsangaben

> **on/onto**
>
> - *on*
>   Beispiel: The milk is <u>on</u> the table.
>
> - *onto*
>   Beispiel: The cat is climbing <u>onto</u> the garage roof.

15. Vervollständige die folgenden Sätze und verwende *on* oder *onto*.

    a) The book is _____ the television.

    b) Mike is lying _____ the floor.

    c) Ruth is throwing her books _____ the table.

    d) Karen is getting off the train _____ the platform.

    e) The dog is sitting _____ the chair.

    f) The dog is jumping _____ the chair.

    g) Davina is carrying her suitcase _____ the train.

    h) George's coat is _____ the bed.

    i) Grandma is walking _____ the grass.

    j) The footballers are running _____ the football field.

16. Übersetze die folgenden Sätze.

    a) Allan steigt in einen Bus ein.
    _____

    b) Mrs Pringle lässt ihre Schlüssel immer auf dem Tisch liegen.
    _____

    c) Oliver geht auf einer Brücke.

    d) Sie laufen auf die Straße.
    _____

... rund ums Nomen: Ortsangaben

to/towards

- *to*
  Beispiel: She drives <u>to</u> work.

- *towards*
  Beispiel: Max is walking <u>towards</u> the cinema.

17. Sieh dir die Bilder genau an und schreibe dazu passende Sätze, wobei du *to* oder *towards* verwendest. Einige nützliche Wörter, die dir bei deinen Antworten helfen können, stehen in Klammern.

a)  Janet _goes to the market_ on Saturdays.

(go / market)

b) 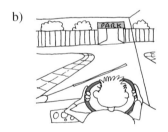 Peter is _____

_____

(drive / park)

c) 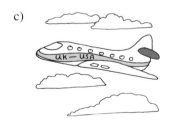 That plane is _____

_____

(fly / America)

65

d) The postman is _____

(walk / the house)

e) The bus is _____

(go)

f) Mr and Mrs Jolly are _____

(read / timetable of the train / Glasgow)

18. Übersetze die folgenden Sätze.

a) Kannst du zum Supermarkt gehen?

b) Carol fährt gerade auf den Bahnhof zu.

c) Valerie und Jeremy gehen (zu Fuß) nach Keswick.

d) Montags geht Peter ins Kino.

... rund ums Nomen: Ortsangaben

* **19. Gemischte Übung:** Das Grab der Königin Hiero
  Die berühmte Archäologin Miss Teek und ihr Assistent Ivor Spade haben beinahe das Rätsel, wie das Grab der Königin zu finden ist, gelöst. Sie haben aber noch ein paar Fragen und brauchen deshalb deine Hilfe. Übersetze die Schriftzeichen links und rechts des Lageplans und du hast die Präpositionen, die du zum Einsetzen in den Text und zum Auffinden des richtigen Planquadrats brauchst, gefunden. Wenn eine Präposition mehr als einmal vorkommt, wird auch das entsprechende Schriftzeichen wiederholt.
  Folgende Präpositionen kommen in dieser Übung vor: *across* (×2), *behind* (×2), *in front of, in the middle, inside, into* (×3), *near, next to* (×2), *on, on the left, on top of, outside, to* (×2), *towards* (×2), *under*.

a)

Go _____ the river and then walk _____ the tree _____ a cave. Five metres _____ the tree _____ a pyramid is the second map. (cave = Höhle)

Frage: In welchem Quadrat befindet sich die zweite Karte? _____

b)

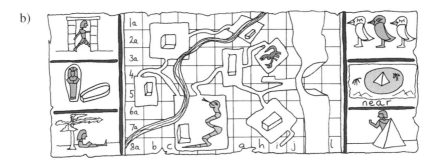

... rund ums Nomen: Ortsangaben

Walk _____ the cave. _____ the cave there is a door _____ a big stone. The stone is _____ of the floor _____ the small river. _____ this door is a third map.

Frage: In welchem Quadrat befindet sich die dritte Karte? _____

c)

Sit _____ the cave in the sunshine. At 6.00 p.m. stand _____ the tree you can see _____. Walk six metres _____ the sun. You are now _____ the entrance _____ the tomb of Empress Hiero.
(entrance = Eingang; tomb = Grab)

Frage: In welchem Quadrat befindet sich der Eingang? _____

d)

Go _____ the entrance and run _____ the room. _____ the wall _____ you are the clues for you to get _____ the treasure room of Empress Hiero.
(clues = Anhaltspunkte/ Schlüssel; treasure room = Schatzkammer)

6.2 Den Weg erklären

Wie erklärst du anderen den Weg?
- In Wegerklärungen verwendest du meist den Imperativ (siehe auch S. 159).
  Beispiele: Turn left.
  Turn right.
  Go straight on.

- Wegerklärungen werden häufig mit Orts- und Richtungsangaben verbunden: *on the left/right, in front of, near, next to, at, into* usw.
  Beispiel: The bus stop is in front of the bank.

- Im Englischen gliederst du längere Wegerklärungen, indem du beispielsweise *first ..., then ..., after that ...* einfügst.
  Beispiel: First go straight on, then turn left, after that turn right, and the shop is on the left.

- Lerne die folgenden Redewendungen auswendig. Dann hast du keine Schwierigkeiten mehr, wenn du einmal nach dem Weg gefragt wirst.

go straight on	Go straight on until the station
	Go straight on past the post office.
turn righ/left	Turn right at the church.
	Turn left down Chester Road.
	Turn left into Park Square.
go across	Go across the market place.
go past	Go past the garage.
go on until	Go on until the station.
take the first (second/third/...)	
	Take the fourth street on the left.

... rund ums Nomen: Ortsangaben

20. Sieh dir die Zeichnung genau an. Ich bin der Autofahrer und du der Fußgänger. Kannst du mir den Weg zu den angegebenen Stellen erklären?

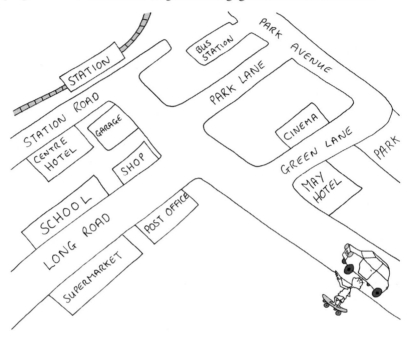

a) (the post office) _First go straight on, then turn left down Long Road and the post office is on the left._

b) (the school) _____

c) (the cinema) _____

d) (the bus station) _____

e) (the park) _____

f) (the Centre Hotel) _____

21. Dies ist eine schwere Übung. Kannst du sie bewältigen? Jasmin und Simon sind auf einem Stadtrundgang durch Castleport. Nach jeder Sehenswürdigkeit, die sie besucht haben, brauchen sie Anweisungen für den Weg zur nächsten, bis sie zum Busbahnhof zurückkehren. Auf der Karte zeigt der Pfeil um jede Zahl, in welche Richtung sie sehen. Du musst jede Wegerklärung von dieser Position aus beginnen.

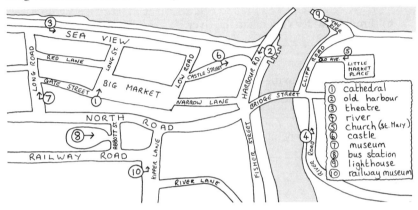

a) From the bus station to the museum.
   First turn left into Abbott Street, then go straight on until North Road. Turn left down North Road and then take the first street right, Long Road, and the museum is on the right.

b) From the museum to the cathedral.

c) From the cathedral to the theatre.

d) From the theatre to the castle.

e) From the castle to the old harbour.

... rund ums Nomen: Ortsangaben

   f) From the old harbour to the lighthouse.
      _____
      _____

   g) From the lighthouse to St. Mary's church.
      _____
      _____

   h) From St. Mary's church to the river.
      _____
      _____

   i) From the river to the railway museum.
      _____
      _____

   j) From the railway museum to the bus station.
      _____
      _____

22. Jasmin und Simon haben sich auch einige andere Dinge in Castleport angesehen. Wenn du meinen Wegerklärungen folgst, kannst du herausfinden, was sie sonst noch besucht haben. Kennzeichne jede Stelle auf der Karte und schreibe den Namen der Straße auf, in der sie sich etwas angesehen haben. Denke daran, dass du immer in Pfeilrichtung beginnen musst.

   a) From the museum.
      Go straight on, then take the second street on the right. The bank is on the right.
      The bank is in:_____

   b) From the theatre.
      Go straight on, then take the first street on the right. Next, turn left into the Big Market and then take the first street on the left. The post office is on the left.
      The post office is in: _____

   c) From the cathedral.
      First turn left, then go straight on, after that turn left and left again. Then, take the second street on the right and the fish shop is on the right past the street on the right.
      The fish shop is in: _____

... rund ums Nomen: Ortsangaben

d) From the river.
First go straight on, then turn left and then right. Next, take the first street on the right, after that go straight on and the café is in front of you. You can't miss it.
The café is in: _____

23. Erkläre, wie jedes Tier sein Lieblingsfressen finden kann, und benutze dafür Imperative.

a) (parrot) *Go straight on to the end. Turn right. Turn left. Take the second left. Take the first right. You're there.*

b) (the dog) _____

c) (the mouse) _____

d) (the cat) _____

e) (the rabbit) _____

... rund ums Nomen: Ortsangaben

24. Für deine Wegerklärungen möchtest du vielleicht noch ein paar neue Wörter lernen, die nützlich für dich sein könnten. Finde aus den Beschreibungen heraus, welche dies sind. Sie haben alle etwas mit Straßen zu tun.

a) On this road you can drive very fast and a long way.

b) Trains go across the road there.

c) These change colour: red, yellow, green.

d) You can go round and round here in a circle.

e) Where roads meet.

f) You can go across the road here on a black and white zoo animal with stripes.

g) You can go under it or over it.

7 Zahlen, Datums- und Zeitangaben

7.1 Grundzahlen

Wann verwendest du Grundzahlen?
Mit **Grundzahlen** gibst du eine **bestimmte Anzahl** und nicht eine bestimmte Reihenfolge an. Eine Grundzahl antwortet dir also auf die Frage "wie viele?".

Welche Grundzahlen gibt es?

1	one	11	eleven	21	twenty-one	90	ninety
2	two	12	twelve	22	twenty-two	100	one hundred
3	three	13	thirteen	23	twenty-three		(a hundred)
4	four	14	fourteen	usw.		200	two hundred
5	five	15	fifteen	30	thirty	300	three hundred
6	six	16	sixteen	40	forty	450	four hundred
7	seven	17	seventeen	50	fifty		and fifty
8	eight	18	eighteen	60	sixty	567	five hundred
9	nine	19	nineteen	70	seventy		and sixty-seven
10	ten	20	twenty	80	eighty	usw.	

1. Mrs Fox, die Mathematiklehrerin, hat einige Rechenaufgaben für dich an die Tafel geschrieben. Schreibe die Zahlen mit den Ergebnissen in Worten auf.

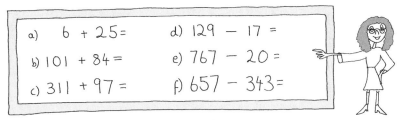

a) 6 + 25 =
b) 101 + 84 =
c) 311 + 97 =
d) 129 − 17 =
e) 767 − 20 =
f) 657 − 343 =

... rund ums Nomen: Zahlen, Datums- und Zeitangaben

a) _six + twenty-five = thirty-one_
b) _____
c) _____
d) _____
e) _____
f) _____

2. Löse das folgende Zahlenrätsel.

across (waagrecht)
1) one hundred and twenty-three
3) seventy-seven
4) six hundred and thirty-one
5) three hundred and eighty-one
7) fifteen
9) four
11) two
13) fourteen
15) two hundred and five
17) eight hundred and ninety-one
18) twelve
19) six hundred and seventy-eight

down (senkrecht)
1) one hundred and three
2) three hundred and sixty-one
3) seven hundred and eleven
6) eighty-five
8) fifty-six
10) twenty-one
12) sixty
14) four hundred and eighty-two
15) two hundred and sixteen
16) five hundred and eighteen

3. Wie heißen diese Zahlen auf Englisch? Schreibe sie in Worten.

a) siebenundzwanzig _seven hundred and twenty_
b) einhundertsechzehn _____
c) dreihundertvierundachtzig _____
d) sechsundzwanzig _____
e) vierhunderteins _____

... rund ums Nomen: Zahlen, Datums- und Zeitangaben

7.2 Ordnungszahlen

Wann verwendest du Ordnungszahlen?
Mit **Ordnungszahlen** gibst du eine **bestimmte Reihenfolge** an.

Welche Ordnungszahlen gibt es?

1st	first	11th	eleventh	30th	thirtieth
2nd	second	12th	twelfth	40th	fortieth
3rd	third	13th	thirteenth	50th	fiftieth
4th	fourth	14th	fourteenth	60th	sixtieth
5th	fifth		usw.	70th	seventieth
6th	sixth	20th	twentieth	80th	eightieth
7th	seventh	21st	twenty-first	90th	ninetieth
8th	eighth	22nd	twenty-second	100th	one hundredth
9th	ninth	23rd	twenty-third		(a hundredth)
10th	tenth	24th	twenty-fourth		usw.

4. Die Einwohner von Plumpton Wood veranstalten jedes Jahr ein Rennen, um zu sehen, wer am schnellsten (oder am listigsten) ist. Aus der Zeichnung kannst du erkennen, in welcher Reihenfolge sie über die Ziellinie laufen. Vervollständige die Anzeigetafel. (Die Wettbewerbsteilnehmer stehen bereits in der richtigen Reihenfolge.)

... rund ums Nomen: Zahlen, Datums- und Zeitangaben

Schreibe, auf welchem Platz sich jeder der folgenden Teilnehmer befindet.

(Schnecke)   _The snail is fifth._

(Maus)

(Schlange)

(Schildkröte)

(Hirsch)

(Katze)

(Spinne)

(Frosch)

(Igel)

(Fuchs)

* 5. Im folgenden Rätsel ist der Name eines berühmten Gebäudes versteckt. Kannst du herausfinden, welches es ist?

links (left)   **rechts** (right)

B V M E L   M B I F W
F S Z G O   S T E E U
E C A Y E   V W G A I
T R U A M   _ _ _   O O A E U
S J A Y M   W X Y G H
F E T D A   _ _ _ _ _ _   H O N P U
I K L H J   F F Q Z S
T G T T I   _ _ _ _ _   P W F I N

78

a) The fifth letter is the thirty-first on the left.
b) The 13th letter is the eighth on the right.
c) The second letter is the twenty-fifth on the right.
d) The ninth letter is the fifth on the left.
e) The 11th letter is the tenth on the left.
f) The 1st letter is the 16th on the left.
g) The twelfth letter is the thirty-seventh on the right.
h) The fourteenth letter is the seventeenth on the left.
i) The eighth letter is the nineteenth on the right.
j) The 3rd letter is the ninth on the right.
k) The 7th letter is the 6th on the left.
l) The sixth letter is the thirty-second on the right.
m) The tenth letter is the 28th on the left.
n) The fourth letter is the eleventh on the left.

6. Kannst du dir ein ähnliches Rätsel für LONDON selbst ausdenken?

7.3 Zeitangaben

Wie gibst du im Englischen an, wie viel Uhr es ist?

Du verwendest für Zeitangaben im Englischen unten stehende Ausdrücke. Mit Ausnahme von *o'clock* werden die Ausdrücke nur gesprochen und nicht geschrieben.

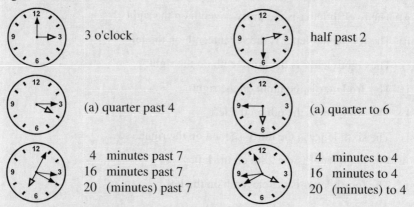

Bei Zeitangaben mit Fünferzahlen kannst du das Wort *minutes* weglassen.

Beispiele: 7.50 = 10 to 8 (ten to eight)
11.05 = 5 past 11 (five past eleven)

7. Schau dir die Uhren an und schreibe dann auf, wie die Zeitangaben gesprochen würden. Wo möglich, lasse *minutes* weg.

... rund ums Nomen: Zahlen, Datums- und Zeitangaben

a) _____
b) _____
c) _____
d) _____
e) _____
f) _____
g) _____
h) _____

Um im Englischen zwischen **Vormittag** und **Nachmittag** zu unterscheiden, musst du *a.m.* (vor Mittag) und *p.m.* (nach Mittag) verwenden.

Beispiele: 2.30 a.m. = 2.30 in the morning
7.45 p.m. = 7.45 in the evening

8. Hier sind die Tätigkeiten und Zeitangaben durcheinander geraten. Bringe sie in die richtige zeitliche Reihenfolge.

... rund ums Nomen: Zahlen, Datums- und Zeitangaben

a) _____

b) _____

c) _____

d) _____

e) *start work after lunch*   *1.20 p.m.*

f) _____

g) _____

h) _____

Bei Fahrplänen (z. B. Zug/Bus/Flugzeug/Schiff) wird gewöhnlich die 24-Stunden-Uhr benutzt. Die Zeitangabe wird in zwei Blöcken gesprochen, ein Block für die Stunden und einer für die Minuten.

Beispiel: 16:56 = sixteen fifty-six

Die Zahl Null in Zeitangaben wird mitgesprochen, und zwar als oh [əu].

Beispiel: 7.05 = seven oh-five

9. Der Fluglotse am Flughafen von Teesside hat heute viel zu tun. Wegen des schlechten Wetters werden viele Flugzeuge nach Teesside umgeleitet. Über Telefon bekommt er die Start- und Landezeiten. Dann muss er diese Informationen an die Ankunfts- und Abflugtafeln schreiben.
Vervollständige die Anzeigetafeln und verwende dazu die durcheinander geratenen Telefonmeldungen.

(departure = **Abflug**)   (arrival = **Ankunft**)

departure: 11 minutes past seven (a.m.), Frankfurt
departure: (a) quarter to eleven (a.m.), Zurich
arrival: ST 926, Paris, nineteen minutes past seven (p.m.)
departure: nine minutes past four (p.m.), Trinidad
arrival: half past ten (a.m.), TWA 114
arrival: JT 784, twenty past six (a.m.)

... rund ums Nomen: Zahlen, Datums- und Zeitangaben

arrival: Oslo, three minutes to twelve (p.m.), SK 555
departure: New York, nine minutes to ten (a.m.)
departure: KLM 456, a quarter past nine (a.m.)
arrival: Madrid, twenty-eight minutes to six (p.m.)

DEPARTURES

BA 3458	FRANKFURT	
KLM 456	AMSTERDAM	
LH 7360		9.51
ZU 2970	ZURICH	
WI 7270	TRINIDAD	

ARRIVALS

	CAIRO	6.20
TWA 1140	CHICAGO	
PA 3350	MADRID	
ST 9260		
	OSLO	

10. Sage die Ankunfts- und Abflugzeiten aus Aufgabe 9 in der zeitlich richtigen Reihenfolge durch und schreibe sie so auf, wie du sie sprechen würdest.

 a) _The plane from Cairo arrives at six twenty._

 b) _The plane to Frankfurt leaves at seven eleven._

 c) _____

 d) _____

 e) _____

 f) _____

 g) _____

 h) _____

 i) _____

 j) _____

... rund ums Nomen: Zahlen, Datums- und Zeitangaben

7.4 Datum

Wie schreibst bzw. sprichst du im Englischen das Datum?

Geschrieben	**Gesprochen**
1st March	the first of March
October 19th	October the nineteenth

Beispiel: John is 12 years old on 22nd June.

Jahreszahlen musst du in zwei Zahlenblöcken lesen.
1997 (19 97) = nineteen ninety-seven, oder folgendermaßen:
nineteen hundred and ninety-seven

Wie heißen die verschiedenen Monate?

Januar	*January*	Februar	*February*
März	*March*	April	*April*
Mai	*May*	Juni	*June*
Juli	*July*	August	*August*
September	*September*	Oktober	*October*
November	*November*	Dezember	*December*

11. Bestimme einige Monatsnamen.

   a) The 3rd month is ___March___.

   b) The 2nd month is _____.

   c) The 9th month is _____.

   d) The 12th month is _____.

   e) The 8th month is _____.

   f) The 4th month is _____.

... rund ums Nomen: Zahlen, Datums- und Zeitangaben

12. Stephen stellt eine Liste mit seinen wichtigen Terminen für das kommende Jahr zusammen, damit seine Mutter sie in ihren Terminkalender eintragen kann. Er hat aber nur in Stichpunkten geschrieben. Kannst du in vollständigen Sätzen ausdrücken, was wann geschehen wird?

a) twenty-first / 1 / Jenny's birthday
   Jenny's birthday is on 21st January .

b) thirteenth / 3 / grandad's birthday
   _____ .

c) seventeenth / 5 / our holiday in Paris
   _____ .

d) thirty-first / 10 / my swimming course
   _____ .

e) second / 11 / my school visit to London
   _____ .

f) fifteenth / 12 / the Christmas concert at the theatre
   _____ .

13. Quiz: Was weißt du über Großbritannien? Wenn du etwas nicht weißt, dann versuche es herauszufinden.

a) When is Halloween?
   Halloween is on 31st October.

b) When is Guy Fawkes Night (Bonfire Night)?
   _____

c) When is New Year's Eve?
   _____

d) When is Boxing Day?
   _____

14. Schreibe in Worten auf, wie du die Geburtsjahre von Simones Verwandten sprechen würdest.

a) _Simone's grandfather_ : _in nineteen fifteen._
b) _____ : _____
c) _____ : _____
d) _____ : _____
e) _____ : _____
f) _____ : _____
g) _____ : _____

7.5 Wochentage

Wie heißen die verschiedenen Wochentage?

Sonntag	*Sunday*	Montag	*Monday*
Dienstag	*Tuesday*	Mittwoch	*Wednesday*
Donnerstag	*Thursday*	Freitag	*Friday*
Samstag	*Saturday*		

15. In dem Bild sind fünf Wochentage versteckt. Ihre Buchstaben sind durcheinander geraten. Kannst du die Buchstaben finden und die Wochentage nennen?

a) _____ b) _____

c) _____ d) _____

e) _____

16. Welche zwei Tage haben in Aufgabe 15 gefehlt?

a) _____ b) _____

17. Wendy und Ian haben beschlossen, dass sie in ihren Ferien in Hunstanton jeden Tag etwas anderes unternehmen wollen. Ian hat alle Prospekte für dich aufgehoben. Was machen sie wann?

Wochentag	**Unternehmung**
Sunday	They go to the circus.

8 Adverbien der Zeit und Häufigkeit

Adverbien drücken aus, **wie etwas getan** wird oder geschieht.

Welche Adverbien der Zeit und Häufigkeit solltest du kennen?
Die wichtigsten Adverbien der Zeit und Häufigkeit sind die folgenden: *always, usually, often, sometimes, never.* Lerne sie auswendig. Du wirst sie oft benötigen.
Beispiel: They sometimes go to the cinema.
Sie gehen manchmal ins Kino.

An welche Stelle im Satz stellst du die Adverbien?
Es gibt zwei Möglichkeiten, die Adverbien der Zeit und Häufigkeit zu stellen:
- unmittelbar **vor** das **Vollverb**
  Beispiel: He often reads a book.

- **zwischen** das **Hilfsverb** und das **Vollverb** (aber nur bei einer zusammengesetzten Zeit) oder **nach einer Form von *to be***
  Beispiele: She can always walk to work.
  He is usually late.

1. Schreibe die folgenden Wörter in der richtigen Reihenfolge, sodass sie Sätze ergeben.

   a) his / bicycle / usually / rides / Peter
   _____

   b) she / plays / tennis / often
   _____

   c) visit / America / in / can / grandma / we / sometimes
   _____

... rund ums Verb: Adverbien der Zeit und Häufigkeit

d) television / Mary / watches / always

e) Lucy / usually / and / sit / together / Susan

f) drives / never / Tony / to / work

g) never / across / the / road / run / must / you

h) swimming / goes / John / sometimes

i) to / Australia / fly / they / often

2. Die folgende Tabelle zeigt, wie oft Henry, Nina, Lucinda und Barry in ihrer Freizeit bestimmte Dinge tun. Schreibe zu jeder Person fünf Sätze und benutze dabei Adverbien der Häufigkeit, um zu zeigen, wie oft sie diese Dinge tun.

▪ = always ▫ = usually ▫ = often

▫ = sometimes ☐ = never

	go to the cinema	watch television	visit a restaurant	go swimming	work with a computer
Henry	often	always	sometimes	never	always
Nina	never	usually	never	often	sometimes
Lucinda	sometimes	often	often	usually	never
Barry	usually	never	sometimes	often	sometimes

Henry

a) *Henry often goes to the cinema.*
b)
c)
d)
e)

Nina

f)
g)
h)
i)
j)

Lucinda

k)
l)
m)
n)
o)

Barry

p)
q)
r)
s)
t)

... rund ums Verb: Adverbien der Zeit und Häufigkeit

Was sind adverbiale Bestimmungen?

Adverbiale Bestimmungen sind zusammengesetzte Ausdrücke, die die gleiche Funktion wie Adverbien haben. Folgende adverbiale Bestimmungen der Zeit und Häufigkeit solltest du in der 5. Klasse kennen: *every morning, every afternoon, every night, every day, on Mondays, on Tuesdays, on ... (days of the week)*.

Beispiel: Every afternoon Jenny plays volleyball.

An welche Stelle im Satz stellst du adverbiale Bestimmungen?

Auch hier hast du zwei Möglichkeiten, die adverbialen Bestimmungen der Zeit und Häufigkeit im Satz unterzubringen.

- **Satzanfang**: Eine adverbiale Bestimmung am **Satzanfang** ist **betonter** als eine am Satzende.

  Beipiel: On Wednesdays William and Tina go to the cinema.

- **Satzende**

  Beispiel: William and Tina go to the cinema on Wednesdays.

3. Schaue dir die folgenden Bilder an und schreibe dann zu jedem einen Satz. Die Verben und Namen, die du brauchst, stehen in Klammern am Ende jeder Zeile. Gib für jede Antwort beide Möglichkeiten an.

a) On Mondays Paula goes to the library.
   (Paula / go)
   Paula goes to the library on Mondays.

b) _____ (Jim / Zoe / eat)
   _____

... rund ums Verb: Adverbien der Zeit und Häufigkeit

c) _____ (Jane / read)

d) _____ (Trevor / wash)

e) _____ (Kim / play)

f) _____ (Carol / Mike / ride)

g) _____ (Peter / make)

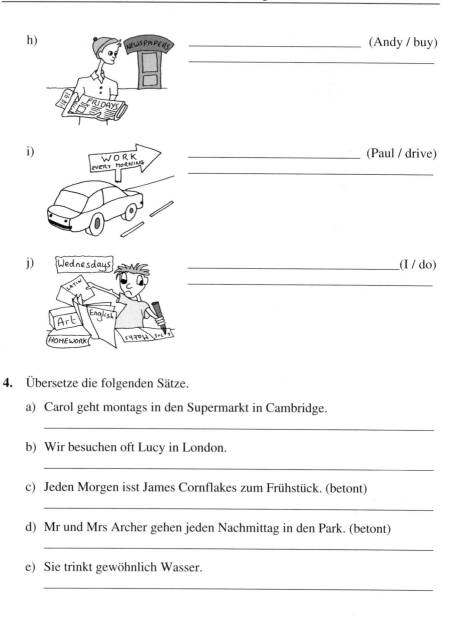

h) _____ (Andy / buy)

i) _____ (Paul / drive)

j) _____ (I / do)

4. Übersetze die folgenden Sätze.

a) Carol geht montags in den Supermarkt in Cambridge.
_____

b) Wir besuchen oft Lucy in London.
_____

c) Jeden Morgen isst James Cornflakes zum Frühstück. (betont)
_____

d) Mr und Mrs Archer gehen jeden Nachmittag in den Park. (betont)
_____

e) Sie trinkt gewöhnlich Wasser.
_____

... rund ums Verb: Adverbien der Zeit und Häufigkeit

✳ **5. Gemischte Übung:** Greg hat einen Geheimcode erfunden, mit dem er seinem Freund mitteilt, was er oder Mitglieder seiner Familie zu bestimmten Zeiten tun.

In jedem Abschnitt der Wörteruhr steht ein Adverb der Häufigkeit oder eine Zeitangabe, wobei die Buchstaben durcheinander geraten sind. Du musst für jeden Satz den passenden Abschnitt der Uhr finden, die Buchstaben in die richtige Reihenfolge bringen und dann den Satz noch einmal schreiben, wobei du das Wort an die richtige Stelle im Satz stellen musst.

Gregs Code funktioniert folgendermaßen: Wenn er z. B. "at 6 o'clock" sagt, ist der richtige Abschnitt auf der Uhr der, der die Nummer 6 umgibt. Wenn der Abschnitt schraffiert ist, soll die Zeitangabe betont sein.

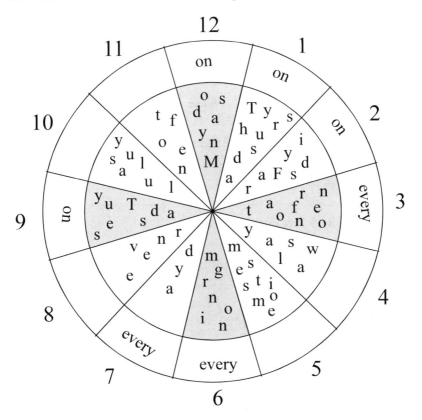

... rund ums Verb: Adverbien der Zeit und Häufigkeit

a) At 4 o'clock I run home from school.
   I always run home from school.

b) At 12 o'clock Laura and I play tennis in Cheltenham.

c) At 7 o'clock I listen to my radio.

d) At 6 o'clock I go swimming before breakfast.

e) I go shopping with my father at 9 o'clock.

f) My sister visits our grandparents at 1 o'clock.

g) My parents take my dog for a walk at 11 o'clock.

h) At 3 o'clock I ride Amanda's horse.

i) At 5 o'clock Aunty Caroline takes June to a football match.

j) I watch television at 8 o'clock.

k) At 2 o'clock I eat my lunch in a café.

l) I can use my sister's bicycle at 10 o'clock.

9 Zeitformen des Verbs

Wenn du sprichst, kannst du von Ereignissen sprechen, die in der Vergangenheit **stattgefunden haben,** die **gerade stattfinden** oder die in der Zukunft **stattfinden werden.** Um diesen Bezug zum Zeitpunkt deines Sprechens auszudrücken, bietet dir die Sprache verschiedene grammatische Zeitformen an: die **Gegenwart,** die Zeiten der **Vergangenheit** und die der **Zukunft.**
Befindet sich ein Geschehen im Verlauf, tritt es gerade ein oder ist es schon abgeschlossen? Hat ein vergangenes Ereignis vielleicht Auswirkungen auf die Gegenwart? Damit du diese Fragen beantworten kannst, brauchst du verschiedene Zeiten der Gegenwart, der Vergangenheit und der Zukunft.

9.1 *simple present*

Wann verwendest du das *simple present*?
Du verwendest das *simple present* (einfaches Präsens) für
- unveränderliche Zustände
  Beispiel: I like cats.
- regelmäßige Ereignisse
  Beispiel: I read books.
- aufeinanderfolgende Handlungen
  Beispiel: First I eat an orange, then I go to school.

... rund ums Verb: Zeitformen des Verbs

Wie bildest du das *simple present*?
- Die Verbform des *simple present* entspricht der des Infinitivs.
  Beispiel: I / You / We / They pl<u>ay</u> golf.
- Die 3. Person Singular wird auf *-s* gebildet.
  Beispiel: He / She / It <u>walks</u> to the park.
  Die Formen der 3. Person Singular lauten:
  read ⟶ read<u>s</u> Verb + *-s* (Normalform)
  teach ⟶ teach<u>es</u> Bei Verben, die auf *ch* enden, wird *-es* angehängt
  (ebenso bei go – go<u>es</u>, do – do<u>es</u>)
  carry ⟶ carr<u>ies</u> Wenn am Ende des Verbs ein Konsonant + *y* steht, so wird das *y* umgewandelt in *i* + *-es*.

1. Vervollständige die folgenden Sätze im *simple present*. Die Verben, die du für die Sätze brauchst, sind in der folgenden Liste durcheinander geraten.
   play / look / like / ride / fly / climb / go / carry / eat / repair / watch / write

   a) Kathy ___plays___ football.
   b) Grandma _____ flowers.
   c) I _____ to London.
   d) They _____ mountains.
   e) Anita _____ apples.
   f) George _____ a suitcase.
   g) We _____ bicycles.
   h) Simon and Fiona _____ an old car.
   i) John _____ to the post office.
   j) Carol _____ television.
   k) You _____ cold.
   l) She _____ songs.

2. Mrs Jones erzählt ihrer Freundin am Telefon, was ihre Familie regelmäßig tut. Kannst du übersetzen, was sie sagt?

a) _____

b) _____

c) _____

Es gibt einige Signalwörter, die dir anzeigen, dass du jetzt das *simple present* verwenden musst: *every day, often, sometimes, never, always, on ...* (z. B. *on Mondays), usually.* Lerne diese Wörter auswendig.

Beispiel: They <u>sometimes</u> <u>go</u> to the theatre.

3. Schau dir die folgenden Bilder genau an und verwende dann ein Verb aus der Liste und das Signalwort aus dem dazugehörigen Bild, um den Satz zu vervollständigen. *make / jog / buy / catch / walk / sleep / go*

a)  Colin *usually*   *makes*   breakfast.

... rund ums Verb: Zeitformen des Verbs

b)  Mary _____ _____ chocolate.

c)  Clive and Jenny _____ _____.

d)  Lucy _____ to the cinema _____.

e)  The dog _____ _____ on a chair.

f)  Amanda _____ _____ a bus to work.

g)  Trevor and Wendy _____ _____ to school.

4. Übersetze, was die Familie Crusoe auf ihrer Insel macht.

a) Wir schwimmen jeden Tag im Meer.
_____

b) Manchmal lese ich eine Zeitung.
_____

c) Wir kochen nie. Wir essen immer im Restaurant.
_____

... rund ums Verb: Zeitformen des Verbs

> Folgende Signalwörter zeigen dir an, dass jetzt mehrere Handlungen aufeinander folgen. Wie du bereits gelernt hast, benutzt du auch dann das *simple present: first ..., then ..., after that ..., next ..., and then ..., soon ..., at last ...*
> Beispiel: First we go to the station, then we catch a train.

5. Vervollständige die folgenden Sätze. Die Verben, die du dazu brauchst, stehen in Klammern am Ende eines jeden Satzes. Aber sie stehen nicht unbedingt in der richtigen Reihenfolge.

   a) First I _____, then I _____ a sauna and after that I _____ home. (have / drive / swim)

   b) First Jenny _____ a book, then she _____ television. (watch / read)

   c) On Mondays, Brian and Arthur _____ tennis, then they _____ in a restaurant. (eat / play)

   d) Every day Karen _____ to the post office, then she _____ for Peter. After that they _____ together to school. (wait / walk / go)

   e) Every morning Paul _____ breakfast and then _____ a newspaper. After that he _____ to work. (go / have / read)

   f) First you _____ the key, then you _____ the door. Next, you _____ the door and then you _____ the light. At last, you _____ inside the house. (be / find / switch on / open / close)

6. Übersetze, was der Frosch sagt.

   Wie überquerst du in England die Straße?
   Sieh erst nach rechts, dann nach links und dann wieder nach rechts, und dann geh über die Straße.

... rund ums Verb: Zeitformen des Verbs

Wenn du einen Satz mit einer **negativen Aussage** formulieren möchtest, musst du nach einer Form von *to be* **not** **hinzufügen**, um den Satz zu verneinen.

Beispiele: She is Karen. She isn't Karen.
She is not Karen.
She's not Karen.

7. Forme die folgenden Sätze in verneinte Sätze um.

   a) Mrs Graham is a teacher.
   Mrs Graham is not a teacher. / Mrs Graham isn't a teacher.

   b) Julie is old.

   c) Martin and Mary are tall.

   d) Mr and Mrs King are American.

   e) I am a doctor.

   f) The bus is white.

   g) We are cooks.

8. Übersetze die folgenden Sätze.

   a) Die Katze ist nicht schwarz.

   b) Ich bin nicht John.

   c) Das sind keine neuen CDs.

... rund ums Verb: Zeitformen des Verbs

Wenn es in einem Satz **keine Form von *to be*** und auch **kein Hilfsverb** (z. B. *can, must, have* usw.) gibt, musst du ***don't/do not*** oder ***doesn't/does not*** (nur in der 3. Person Singular) **einfügen,** um den Satz zu verneinen.

Beispiele: I read books.   I don't read books.
She eats apples.   She doesn't eat apples.

9. Schau dir die folgenden Zeichnungen an und schreibe dann acht passende verneinte Sätze. Ersetze in deinen Antworten vorkommende Namen durch Personalpronomen.

a) _He doesn't want a bike._

b) _____

c) _____

d) _____

e) _____

f) _____

g) _____

h) _____

10. Großtante June muss heute die Haustiere der Familie versorgen, hat aber vergessen, wer was frisst. Übersetze, was die Haustiere sagen.

a) _____

b) _____

c) _____

11. Gemischte Übung: Der Fremdenführer auf Morton Manor erzählt den Besuchern nie die Wahrheit über das Haus. Es ist sogar so, dass alles, was er sagt, falsch ist. Schreibe seine Erklärungen so um, dass sie stimmen. Verwende dazu korrekte Verneinungsformen.

a) *Morton Manor isn't 70 meters high.*

b) _____

c) _____

d) _____

e) _____

f) _____

g) _____

h) _____

i) _____

... rund ums Verb: Zeitformen des Verbs

Du kannst **Fragesätze** bilden, indem du *do/does* verwendest.

Beispiele: <u>Do</u> I / you / we / you / they play tennis?
<u>Does</u> he / she / it play tennis?
I / You / We / You / They play tennis. (bejahter Satz)
He / She / It plays tennis. (bejahter Satz)

Die Satzstellung sieht folgendermaßen aus. Präge sie dir gut ein!

do/does + Subjekt + Verb + Objekt

Beispiel: <u>Does</u> <u>he</u> <u>like</u> <u>chocolate</u>?

Beachte: Das Verb steht in der Infinitiv-Form, aber es steht kein *to* dabei. Dies gilt auch für die 3. Person Singular (he/she/it).

12. Mark fährt das erste Mal mit einem Zug. Vervollständige die Fragen, die er stellt. Benutze dazu folgende Verben: *buy / stop / sit / go* (× 2) */ wear / use / have*

a) _____ we _____ a ticket here?

b) _____ the train _____ fast?

c) _____ it _____ to London?

d) _____ many people _____ the train?

e) _____ we _____ at York?

f) _____ I _____ here?

g) _____ the train driver _____ a uniform?

h) _____ the train _____ a restaurant?

Auf Fragen mit *do/does* kannst du **Kurzantworten** geben. Diese werden so gebildet:

<u>Do</u> I / you / we / you / they ...? <u>No</u>, I / you / we / you / they <u>don't</u>.
<u>Yes</u>, I / you / we / you / they <u>do</u>.

<u>Does</u> he / she / it ...? <u>No</u>, he / she / it <u>doesn't</u>.
<u>Yes</u>, he / she / it <u>does</u>.

... rund ums Verb: Zeitformen des Verbs

13. Die Klasse 5 b wird bald zu einem Schüleraustausch nach Großbritannien fahren. Die Schüler haben viele Fragen an ihren Lehrer. Kannst du die Fragen vervollständigen und passende Kurzantworten darauf geben?

a)    _Do_ you _stay_ with a family, too?
   Yes, I do. (ja)

b) 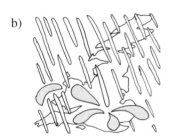   _____ it always _____ in Great Britain?
   _____ (nein)

c)    _____ I _____ an umbrella?
   _____ (ja)

d)    _____ we _____ Manchester?
   _____ (nein)

... rund ums Verb: Zeitformen des Verbs

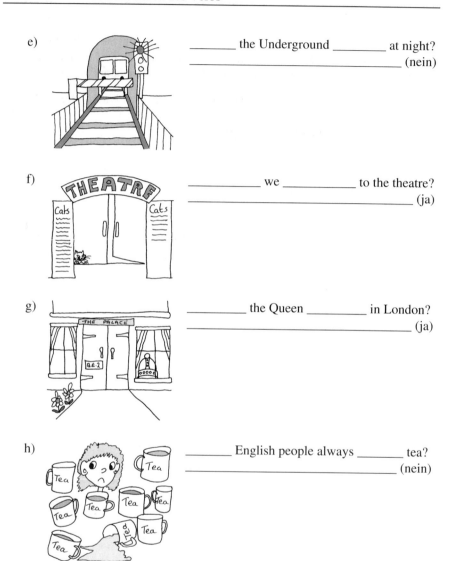

e) _____ the Underground _____ at night?
_____ (nein)

f) _____ we _____ to the theatre?
_____ (ja)

g) _____ the Queen _____ in London?
_____ (ja)

h) _____ English people always _____ tea?
_____ (nein)

9.2 present progressive

Wann verwendest du das *present progressive*?
Du benutzt das *present progressive* (Verlaufsform der Gegenwart), um auszudrücken, was **zum Zeitpunkt des Sprechens gerade geschieht.**
Beispiel: She is writing a letter.   Sie schreibt gerade einen Brief.

Wie bildest du das *present progressive*?

read → reading		Im Normalfall: Verb + *-ing*
run → ru**nn**ing		Wenn der vorausgehende Vokal kurz ist und die letzte Silbe betont wird: Verdoppelung des Konsonanten.
write → writing		Wenn das Verb mit einem *-e* endet, so fällt dieses weg.
lie → lying		Aus *-ie* am Ende des Verbs wird *-y*.

14. Hier sind ein paar deutsche Verben, bei denen die Buchstaben durcheinander geraten sind. Schreibe das englische Wort in das Rad und schreibe danach auch noch die Verlaufsform des englischen Verbs auf.

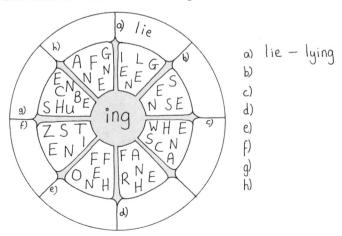

a) lie – lying
b)
c)
d)
e)
f)
g)
h)

15. Es sind Ferien auf Middleton Castle. Was tut jeder gerade?

a) The guards are ___sleeping___.

b) The king _____.

c) The queen _____.

d) _____ princes _____ kites.

e) _____ princess _____.

f) _____ a boat.

g) The musicians _____ tennis.

16. Übersetze die folgenden Sätze.

a) Heute regnet es.

_____

b) Debbie sitzt auf einem Stuhl.

_____

c) Sie machen gerade das Frühstück.

_____

... rund ums Verb: Zeitformen des Verbs

Verneinte Sätze, in denen das *present progressive* verwendet wird, bildest du, indem du *not* **zwischen die Form von** *to be* **und Verb + -*ing* setzt.

Beispiel: She isn't singing. (Langform: She is not singing.)

Wenn du diese Form benutzt, kannst du sagen, was gerade **nicht** passiert.

17. Schau dir die Bilder genau an und schreibe dann, was gerade nicht passiert.

a)  It _isn't snowing._

b)  They _____

c)  She _____

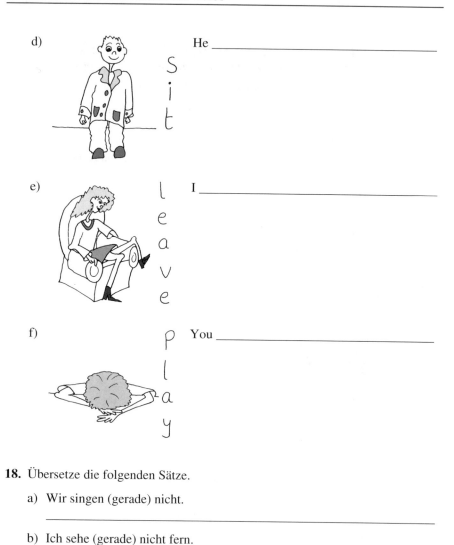

d) He _____

e) I _____

f) You _____

18. Übersetze die folgenden Sätze.

a) Wir singen (gerade) nicht.

_____

b) Ich sehe (gerade) nicht fern.

_____

c) Sie rennt (gerade) nicht.

_____

... rund ums Verb: Zeitformen des Verbs

Mit dem *present progressive* kannst du **Fragen** zu dem stellen, was zum Zeitpunkt des Sprechens gerade passiert. Benutze dazu die folgende Satzstellung:

eine Form von *to be* + Subjekt + Verb + *-ing* + Objekt

Beispiel: Are   you   cleaning   the car?

19. Schau dir die Bilder genau an und bilde eine passende Frage zu dem, was die Leute gerade machen.

a) *Are you washing the window?*

b)  Am I _____ in a mirror?

c) Is _____

113

... rund ums Verb: Zeitformen des Verbs

d)  _____

e)  _____

f)  _____

g)  _____

... rund ums Verb: Zeitformen des Verbs

Auf Entscheidungsfragen im *present progressive* werden gewöhnlich **Kurzantworten** gegeben.

Beispiel: Are they leaving the party?   Yes, they are.
No, they aren't.
(No, they're not.)

20. Benutze das Bild, um die folgenden Fragen zu stellen. Gib auch eine passende Antwort.

a) _____ the man _____ potatoes? No, _____.
b) _____ the two women _____ for a bus? _____.
c) _____ the girl _____ a bicycle? _____.
d) _____ the boy _____ photos? _____.
e) _____ sleeping? _____.

21. Kannst du jetzt die entgegengesetzten Kurzantworten wie bei Übung 20 aufschreiben?

a) *Yes, he is.*
b) _____
c) _____
d) _____
e) _____

... rund ums Verb: Zeitformen des Verbs

22. Gemischte Übung: Setze die fehlenden Verben in der richtigen Form ein.

a) I _like_ snow but today it _is raining_ . (like / rain)

b) Jenny _____ at the George Hotel. She usually _____ at the King's Head Hotel. (stay / stay)

c) Sarah _____ a picture now and never _____ books. (paint / read)

d) Uncle Henry _____ in America and today grandma _____ to him. (live / write)

e) Julie and I always _____ the theatre on Saturdays. Today, we _____ 'Cats'. (visit / watch)

f) The suitcase _____ clean, but it _____ old. (be / get)

g) The dog _____ at the door, it _____ its dinner. (bark / want)

23. Gemischte Übung: Vervollständige die folgende Comic-Zeichnung. Die Verben, die du dafür brauchst, sind durcheinander gemischt im letzten Kasten.

24. Gemischte Übung: Wer wohnt wo?
Vervollständige die folgenden Hinweise und entscheide, ob du das *simple present* oder das *present progressive* brauchst. Die Verben, die du dazu brauchst, sind im Wald am Ende von Wood Lane.

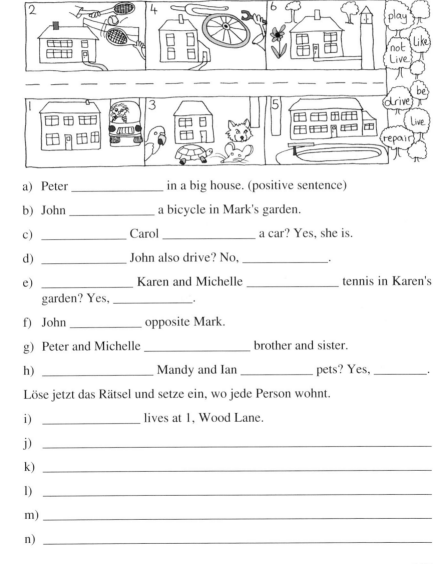

a) Peter _____ in a big house. (positive sentence)

b) John _____ a bicycle in Mark's garden.

c) _____ Carol _____ a car? Yes, she is.

d) _____ John also drive? No, _____.

e) _____ Karen and Michelle _____ tennis in Karen's garden? Yes, _____.

f) John _____ opposite Mark.

g) Peter and Michelle _____ brother and sister.

h) _____ Mandy and Ian _____ pets? Yes, _____.

Löse jetzt das Rätsel und setze ein, wo jede Person wohnt.

i) _____ lives at 1, Wood Lane.

j) _____

k) _____

l) _____

m) _____

n) _____

9.3 simple past

Wann verwendest du das *simple past*?
Du verwendest das *simple past*, wenn du von **abgeschlossenen Handlungen** und Zuständen berichten willst.

Wie bildest du das *simple past*?

repair →	repair<u>ed</u>	Verb + *-ed* (Normalfall)
arrive →	arriv<u>ed</u>	An Verben, die auf ein stummes *-e* enden, wird *-d* angehängt.
jog →	jogg<u>ed</u>	Nach einem kurzen einfachen Vokal wird der Endkonsonant verdoppelt und *-ed* angehängt.
cry →	cr<u>ied</u>	Wenn am Ende des Verbs ein Konsonant + *y* steht, so wird das *y* umgewandelt in *i + ed*.

Die Form des *simple past* ist für alle Personen gleich.

25. Vervollständige die folgende Tabelle.

Deutsch		**Englisch**
Verb	**Infinitiv des Verbs**	**past tense**
schließen	_close_	_closed_
malen		
anrufen		
versuchen		
spielen		
reparieren		
trocknen		
halten		
nutzen		

26. Sheila Lock-Holmes, die berühmte Detektivin, hat von einem Einbruch in Holkham Hall Beweise gesammelt. Vervollständige ihren Bericht mithilfe der Zeichnungen, die sie in ihr Notizbuch gemacht hat.

a) The burglars ___walked___ to the house.

b) One burglar, the woman, _____ through a window.

c) Then, she _____ the door for the man.

d) She _____ the telephone.

e) She _____ the money to their car.

f) They _____ the burglary on 6th January.

g) They _____ their car next to the bus stop.

27. Übersetze die folgenden Sätze.

a) Colin ging zu Fuß zur Arbeit.

b) Kim zog in ein neues Haus.

c) Gill rief am Montag ihren Freund an.

d) Julie und Katie gefielen ihre Ferien in Irland.

... rund ums Verb: Zeitformen des Verbs

> Die Vergangenheitsformen von *to be* lauten *was* und *were*.
> *Beispiele:*   I / He / She / It <u>was</u> in America.
>   You / We / You / They <u>were</u> in England.

28. Forme die Sätze um und benutze das *simple past*.

a) He is in the kitchen.
   He was in the kitchen.

b) I am a teacher.

c) She is outside the shop.

d) They are on holiday.

e) We are happy.

f) You are in front of the post office.

g) I am ready to go to school.

h) She is with Jane.

29. Übersetze die folgenden Sätze.

a) Sally war im Garten.

b) Charles und Rebecca waren gute Freunde.

c) Das Auto war grün.

... rund ums Verb: Zeitformen des Verbs

Die Vergangenheitsform von *has/have* lautet *had*.
Beispiele: I / You / He / She / It / We / You / They had a walk yesterday.
had ist auch die Vergangenheitsform von *have got/has got*.
Beispiel: He had a car.

30. Setze die folgenden Sätze ins *simple past*.

a) Geoff has sandwiches for his dinner.
Geoff had sandwiches for his dinner.

b) Julie has a holiday in Ely.
_____

c) I have cornflakes for breakfast.
_____

d) Every day they have a walk in the park.
_____

e) We have two pizzas in our car.
_____

31. Tina hat einige alte Fotos von ihrer Familie und von Freunden gefunden. Mit was sind sie auf den Fotos abgelichtet worden?

121

... rund ums Verb: Zeitformen des Verbs

a) *Linda had a horse.*
b) _____
c) _____
d) _____

32. Übersetze die folgenden Sätze.

a) Lucy hatte eine alte Zeitschrift.
_____

b) Arnold hatte gestern Geburtstag.
_____

Viele englische Verben haben im *past tense* eine **unregelmäßige Form**.

Beispiele: be   ⟶   was/were
           has/have ⟶   had
           do/does   ⟶   did

Lerne die Formen der unregelmäßigen Verben, die in deinem Englischbuch stehen, auswendig.

Beachte: *did* ist das *simple past* von *do/does*. Es ist für alle Personen gleich.
Beispiel: I / You / He / She / It / We / You / They did all the work.

33. Schreibe die Formen des *simple past* neben die Infinitive. Falls du einige nicht kennst, kannst du sie in dem Puzzle finden. Bis auf eine Form fangen alle mit demselben Buchstaben an wie der Infinitiv und viele sind Infinitiven sehr ähnlich.

```
C W S T M E
A E A H A W
M N W O D R
E T P U E O
(B O U G H T)
G O T H M E
P K T T O D
```

buy   *bought*_____   see   _____
come _____   take _____
get   _____   think _____
go   _____   write _____
make _____
put   _____

122

... rund ums Verb: Zeitformen des Verbs

34. Ian und Barbara sind letzte Woche in den Skiurlaub gefahren. Vervollständige die Sätze mit den unregelmäßigen Verben, die du bis jetzt in diesem Buch gelernt hast.

a) They _____ by train.

b) They _____ to Scotland.

c) Barbara _____ a suitcase with her.

d) Ian _____ a kilt.

e) Ian and Barbara _____ the Loch Ness Monster!

f) They _____ a lot of photographs.

g) Barbara _____ many new friends.

h) Ian _____ Scotland _____ beautiful.

i) They _____ a lot of fun.

j) Ian and Barbara _____ home on Saturday.

k) Barbara _____ two postcards to her friends.

l) They _____ a nice holiday.

m) Ian _____ snow in Barbara's hat.

n) She _____ ill on Monday.

o) They _____ to Aberdeen and _____ new ski gloves.

p) Ian _____ a lot of reading.

35. Am ersten sonnigen Tag des Jahres taten die sieben Nachbarn in der Clifton Street alle etwas anderes. Kannst du sagen, was jede Person getan hat?

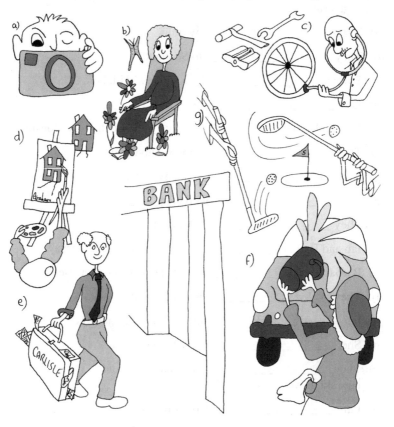

a) Mr Brown ____took photos._____
b) Mrs Fisher _____ in her garden.
c) Dr. Carter _____ his bicycle.
d) Miss Graham _____
e) Mr Carlisle _____
f) Mrs Masters _____
g) Mr and Mrs Cox _____

9.4 *going-to-future*

Wann verwendest du das *going-to-future*?
Du verwendest das *going-to-future*, um **Pläne und Absichten in der Zukunft** auszudrücken.
Beispiel: I am <u>going to</u> read my book.   Ich werde mein Buch lesen.

Wie bildest du das *going-to-future*?
Präsens von *to be* + *going to* + Grundform des Verbs (Infinitiv)
Beispiel: She is <u>going to</u> visit her friends.

Die Verneinung bildest du, indem du *not* einfügst:
Präsens von *to be* + *not going to* + Grundform des Verbs (Infinitiv)
Beispiel: They are <u>not going to</u> go to Wales.
(They aren't going to go to Wales.)

36. Die Klasse 5 c hat geplant, für ein langes Wochenende nach Paris zu fahren. Was beabsichtigen sie zu tun?

a)

We   *are going to fly to Paris.*

b)

We _____

... rund ums Verb: Zeitformen des Verbs

c) She _____

d) He _____

e) I _____

f) They _____

37. Mrs Archer möchte in ihrer Familie einiges verändern. Welche Dinge werden die Familienmitglieder ihrer Vorstellung nach nicht mehr tun?

a) We're not going to use the car.
b) _____
c) _____
d) _____
e) _____
f) _____
g) _____

38. Übersetze die folgenden Sätze.

a) _____
b) _____
c) _____

... rund ums Verb: Zeitformen des Verbs

Fragen zu zukünftigen Plänen und Absichten bildest du mit einer Form von *to be* und *going to*:
(Fragewort +) Form von *to be* + Subjekt + *going to* + Grundform des Verbs + Objekt

Beispiele: What is he going to read?
Is she going to buy a car?

Antworten auf Entscheidungsfragen mit *going to* können ganz kurz sein oder ausführlicher. Dann enthalten sie zusätzliche Informationen.

Beispiele: Are they going to visit Mary?
Yes, they are./No, they aren't. (No, they're not.)
Is he going to play tennis?
Yes he is. But first he's going to meet Jane.
No, he isn't. (No, he's not.) He's going to go to the cinema.

39. Bilde *going-to*-Fragen mithilfe der Informationen in den Klammern.

a) _Is he going to ride his bicycle?_ (he / ride / bicycle)
b) _____ (they / drive / car)
c) _____ (she / buy / camera)
d) _____ (it / rain / tomorrow)
e) _____ (we / stay / John's house)
f) _____ (they / sell / house)
g) _____ (she / lock / door)
h) _____ (he / clean / floor)
i) _____ (they / fly / Japan)
j) _____ (we / go / skiing)
k) _____ (you / read / book)
l) _____ (it / work / today)
m) _____ (she / eat / cake)

... rund ums Verb: Zeitformen des Verbs

40. Die Fragen von a bis f in Übung 39 sind in Bildern beantwortet worden. Beantworte die Fragen und schreibe die verneinten Antworten ausführlicher. Die entsprechenden Bilder helfen dir dabei.

a) *No, he isn't. He's going to paint it.*

b) _____

c) _____

d) _____

e) _____

f) _____

41. Übersetze die folgenden Fragen und Antworten.

a)

... rund ums Verb: Zeitformen des Verbs

10 Hilfsverben

Hilfsverben können – im Gegensatz zu Vollverben – nicht alleine stehen, sondern immer nur zusammen mit einem anderen Verb einem Adjektiv oder einem Nomen. Daher auch der Name 'Hilfs'verb.

10.1 *to be*

Welche Formen kann *to be* haben?
Die Kurzformen verwendet man im gesprochenen Englisch besonders oft.
Beide Formen sind aber gleichermaßen richtig.

Langform	**Kurzform**
I am	I'm
you are	you're
he / she / it is	he's / she's / it's
we / you / they are	we're / you're / they're

Beispiel: I <u>am</u> John Smith. **Aber auch:** I'<u>m</u> John Smith

1. Bilde mit den angegebenen Wörtern zu jedem Bild Sätze.

a)  The bird is small.
It is small.
The bird is black.
It's black.
(small / black)

... rund ums Verb: Hilfsverben

b) _____
_____
_____
_____
(pretty / thin)

c) _____
_____
_____
_____
(new / big)

d) _____
_____
_____
_____
(mouse / white)

e) _____
_____
_____
_____
(beautiful / red)

... rund ums Verb: Hilfsverben

2. Übersetze, was die berühmte Popgruppe 'UR11' über sich erzählt.

a) _____
b) _____
c) _____
d) _____
e) _____

> Wenn du einen Satz mit einer **negativen Aussage** formulieren möchtest, musst nach einer Form von *to be* **not einfügen,** um den Satz zu verneinen.
>
> *Beispiele:*   She <u>is</u> Karen.   She <u>isn't</u> Karen.
>   She <u>is not</u> Karen.
>   She<u>'s not</u> Karen.

3. Vervollständige die folgenden Sätze mit einer verneinten Form von *to be*.

a) He _____ small.   b) We _____ in a café.

c) They _____ boys.   d) I _____ English.

e) You _____ old.   f) She _____ happy.

... rund ums Verb: Hilfsverben

4. Schau dir die Bilder an und bilde dann Sätze mit bejahten und verneinten Aussagen.

a)  (footballer)

She isn't a footballer.
She's a horserider.

b)  (doctor)

c)  (dancers)

d)  (cooks)

... rund ums Verb: Hilfsverben

Du bildest **Fragesätze mit** *to be,* indem du die Form von *to be* an den Anfang des Satzes stellst. **Kurzantworten** auf die Fragen mit *to be* sind ebenso möglich. Aber Achtung: Wenn du mit 'ja' antwortest, darfst du die Kurzform von *to be* nicht verwenden.

Beispiel: Are they from America?   No, they are not.
                                      No, they aren't.
                                      No, they're not.
                                      Yes, they are.

5. Beantworte die folgenden Fragen.
   a) Is he George Black? _____ (nein)
   b) Is she a teacher? _____ (ja)
   c) Are you German? _____ (ja)
   d) Is it a big dog? _____ (nein)
   e) Are we friends? _____ (ja)

6. Falsch verbunden: Kannst du die passenden Antworten auf die Fragen finden? Zuerst musst du die Verben finden, die bei der falschen Vermittlung verloren gegangen sind.

a) _____
b) _____
c) _____
d) _____
e) _____

10.2 have/has got

Wann verwendest du *have/has got* und welche Formen kann *have/has got* haben?

Du benutzt *have/has got* in Aussagesätzen um auszudrücken, was jemand besitzt.

Langform
I / you / we / you / they have got
he / she / it has got

Kurzform
I've / you've / we've / you've / they've got
he's / she's / it's got

Beispiel: We <u>have got</u> a new car. **Aber auch:** We<u>'ve got</u> a new car.

7. Sieh dir das Bild genau an und vervollständige die Sätze mit einer Form von *have/has got*.

a) June und Ivor <u>have got ice-creams.</u>

b) Janet and John _____

c) Peter_____

d) Lucy and Rebecca_____

e) Rachel _____

f) Wendy_____

... rund ums Verb: Hilfsverben

8. Carol hat ein paar eigenartige neue Nachbarn. Übersetze, was sie über sie sagt.

a) Sie haben Hüte und Sonnenbrillen.

b) Sie hat einen Hund und ein Krokodil.

c) Er hat große Füße.

Du bildest **verneinte Aussagesätze mit** *have/has got*, indem du *not* zwischen *have/has* und *got* einfügst.

Langform
I / you / we / you / they have not got
he / she / it has not got

Kurzform
I / you / we / you / they haven't got
he / she / it hasn't got

Beispiel: He <u>has</u> not <u>got</u> a new car. He <u>hasn't</u> <u>got</u> a new car.

9. Schreibe passende Sätze mit *haven't/hasn't got*.

a) I haven't got a dog.

b) she

c) we

d) they

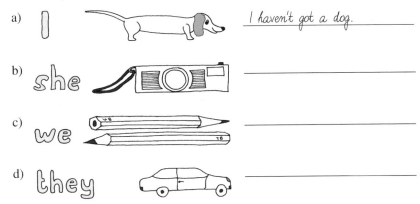

... rund ums Verb: Hilfsverben

10. Für die Übung 11 benötigst du einige Wörter, die du hier schon einmal lernen kannst. Schreibe die englischen Wörter auf, die zu diesen Umrissen gehören.

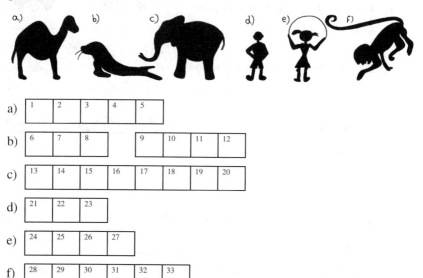

a) | 1 | 2 | 3 | 4 | 5 |

b) | 6 | 7 | 8 | | 9 | 10 | 11 | 12 |

c) | 13 | 14 | 15 | 16 | 17 | 18 | 19 | 20 |

d) | 21 | 22 | 23 |

e) | 24 | 25 | 26 | 27 |

f) | 28 | 29 | 30 | 31 | 32 | 33 |

Hier sind Bezeichnungen für einige Körperteile, die du auch für die nächste Übung benötigst. Die Zahl in jedem Kästchen steht für einen Buchstaben aus dem Umriss-Rätsel.

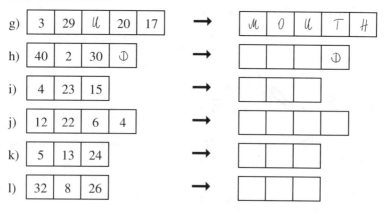

11. Der Person, die die Bilder gezeichnet hat, sind ein paar Fehler unterlaufen. Kannst du ihr sagen, was sie falsch gemacht hat, indem du eine Form von *haven't got* benutzt?

a) *The camel hasn't got a mouth.*
b)
c)
d)
e)
f)

Du bildest **Fragesätze mit *have/has got*,** indem du *have/has* an den Anfang des Satzes und *got* zwischen Subjekt und Objekt stellst.

Beispiel: <u>Have</u> you <u>got</u> a dog?

Bei **Kurzantworten** auf die Fragen mit *have/has got* musst du das *got* wegfallen lassen.

Beispiel: Has Lucy got a red coat? Yes, she <u>has</u>.
No, she <u>hasn't</u>.

... rund ums Verb: Hilfsverben

12. Die Bilder führen dich zu den Wörtern, die du brauchst, um die *have/has got*-Fragen zu vervollständigen. Schreibe auch die passenden Kurzantworten dazu auf.

a)  (door)
Has the house got a door?
No, it hasn't.

b)  (dog)
___ Mr and Mrs Smith_____?
Yes, _____

c)  (long hair)
___ the girls _____?
_____

d)  (book)

e)  (radio)

... rund ums Verb: Hilfsverben

f) (boat)

g) (train)

h) (plant)

i) (telephone)

j) (balls)

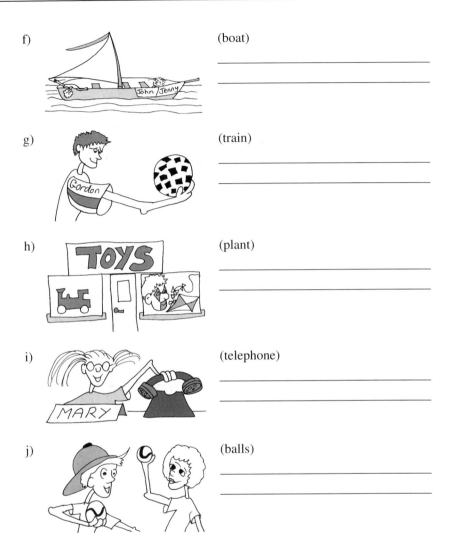

13. In der Entwicklungsabteilung der 'Höhlenmenschen GmbH' versuchen Torc, Hull und Withwords immer neue Erfindungen zu machen. Kannst du die Sätze mit einer Form von *have/has got* vervollständigen? In einigen Fällen musst du auch ein Subjekt ergänzen.

10.3 Die modalen Hilfsverben *can*, *may*, *must* und *have*

Wann verwendest du die modalen Hilfsverben *can*, *may*, *must* und *have*?
Mit den **modalen Hilfsverben** kannst du ganz bestimmte **Sprechabsichten** ausdrücken.

- *can*
  Du benutzt *can*, wenn du ausdrücken willst, dass etwas möglich ist oder dass jemand die **Fähigkeit** besitzt, etwas Bestimmtes zu tun. Bei Verneinungen wird im gesprochenen und geschriebenen Englisch häufig die Kurzform *can't* verwendet.
  Beispiel: She <u>can</u> drive a bus.   She <u>can't</u> (<u>cannot</u>) ride a bike.

14. Was können Julian und seine Freunde tun? Schreibe noch jeweils einen zweiten Satz, in dem du das Subjekt durch das passende Personalpronomen ersetzt.

a) <u>Julian can fly a plane.</u>
   <u>He can fly a plane.</u>

b) Mike and Sylvia _____

c) Amanda and Gary _____

d) Gary _____

e) Sylvia _____

... rund ums Verb: Hilfsverben

15. Sieh dir noch einmal Übung 14 an. Schreibe Sätze über das, was Julian und seine Freunde nicht tun können. Wo es möglich ist, stelle eine Gruppe von Leuten zusammen, die die gleiche Tätigkeit nicht ausüben können.

a) _Mike, Amanda, Gary and Sylvia can't fly a plane._
b) _____
c) _____
d) _____
e) _____

16. Auf dieser Graffitiwand stehen acht *can*-Fragen, aber die Satzstellung ist durcheinander geraten. Kannst du die Fragen richtig stellen?

a) _Can they ride bikes?_
b) _____
c) _____
d) _____
e) _____
f) _____
g) _____
h) _____

... rund ums Verb: Hilfsverben

17. In den Luftballons des Clowns befinden sich die Antworten auf die Fragen, die du gerade in Übung 16 gestellt hast. Sie stehen in der richtigen Reihenfolge von links nach rechts, aber du musst die Kurzantworten noch ausformulieren.

   a) *No, they can't.*
   b) _____
   c) _____
   d) _____
   e) _____
   f) _____
   g) _____
   h) _____

- **may**
  may gebrauchst du, um nach **Erlaubnis** zu fragen oder eine Erlaubnis zu erteilen und um **Hilfe** anzubieten. Es gibt **keine Kurzform** von *may not*.
  Beispiele: May I have a glass of water? Yes, you may./No, you may not.
  May I help you?

18. Bilde Aussagesätze mit *may*. Verwende dafür die Informationen in den Klammern.

   a) *Martin and Kim may make breakfast.*
      (Martin/Kim: make breakfast)
   b) _____
      (Jacky: close the window)
   c) _____
      (Peter: go to the shop)

... rund ums Verb: Hilfsverben

    d) _____
       (Jenny: buy a new dress)
    e) _____
       (Carol/Lucy: go to the pop concert)
    f) _____
       (Ian: visit his friend)

19. Heute hat Kathy Geburtstag und sie hat alle ihre Freunde zum Tee eingeladen. Was fragen ihre Freunde auf der Party? Die Gegenstände findest du auf dem Bild. Die Verben und Subjekte der Sätze stehen in Klammern.

    a) _____ (open / we)
    b) _____ (have / I)
    c) _____ (eat / Kim)
    d) _____ (have / Tim and Jenny)
    e) _____ (use / Becky)
    f) _____ (drink / Robert and I)
    g) _____ (eat / I)
    h) _____ (play / we)

... rund ums Verb: Hilfsverben

20. Vervollständige die folgenden Sätze mit *can* oder *may*.

   a) _____ James speak German?
   b) _____ I go to the disco?
   c) _____ I have an ice-cream?
   d) _____ Francis make ice-cream?
   e) _____ we visit London, please?
   f) _____ I go with you?
   g) _____ I listen to your new CD?
   h) _____ you help me?
   i) _____ I help you?
   j) _____ Georgina read your book?

21. Die Antworten auf die Fragen in Übung 20 sind durcheinander geraten. Versuche, zu jeder Frage die richtige Antwort herauszuarbeiten.

   a) *Yes, he can.*   b) _____
   c) _____   d) _____
   e) _____   f) _____
   g) _____   h) _____
   i) _____   j) _____

147

- **must**

  must wird benutzt, wenn etwas **verpflichtend** oder **notwendig** ist. Um auszudrücken, was man nicht tun darf, verwendet man *must not*. Gewöhnlich wird die Kurzform *mustn't* gebraucht.

  Beispiel: I must phone my mother.

  Verneinte Antworten auf Fragen mit *must* werden gewöhnlich mit *need not (needn't)* und nicht mit *must not (mustn't)* gebildet. *Must not* ist ein sehr strenges Verbot.

  Beispiel: Must you write the letter now? No, I needn't.

22. John, Tina, Mary und Tom planen einen Tagesausflug. Erkläre, was sie vor ihrem Ausflug erst noch tun müssen. Benutze in deinen Sätzen Personalpronomen.

    a) *"I must make sandwiches."*
       (John – make sandwiches)

    b) _____
       (Mary – find my umbrella)

    c) _____
       (Tina/Tom – buy a bottle of water)

    d) _____
       (to Mary/Tina – bring a map)

    e) _____
       (Mary/John – take our cameras)

23. Sieh dir die folgenden Bilder an und entscheide, was nicht geschehen darf.

    a)  You _____

... rund ums Verb: Hilfsverben

b) She _____

c) They _____

d) He _____

24. Die Familie Watson plant, in den Ferien nach Deutschland zu fahren. Mr und Mrs Watsons Kinder Susie und Harry wollen viel wissen. Kannst du ihre Fragen anhand der Informationen in den Klammern und der Bilder stellen?

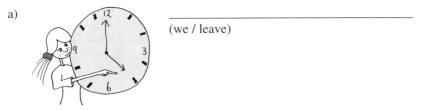

a) _____
(we / leave)

... rund ums Verb: Hilfsverben

b) _____ (I / take)

c) _____ (Susie / sit)

d) _____ (we / stay awake)

e) _____ (dad / drive)

f) _____ (you / make)

... rund ums Verb: Hilfsverben

25. Mr und Mrs Watson beantworten die Fragen ihrer Kinder, indem sie ein Bild zeichnen. Der erste Buchstabe der jeweiligen Antwort steht von rechts nach links in der richtigen Reihenfolge. Kannst du sie richtig schreiben?

a) _____   b) _____

c) _____   d) _____

e) _____   f) _____

26. Vervollständige die folgenden Fragen mit *can* oder *must*.

a) _____ you meet me at 2.00 p.m.?

b) _____ Lucy swim?

c) _____ Henry always brings his friend?

d) _____ Ivor paint the wall blue?

e) _____ I be quiet?

f) _____ we buy Karen a present today?

g) _____ I tell grandad my story, it's boring?

h) _____ you mend my car?

i) _____ you use the other door, please?

... rund ums Verb: Hilfsverben

27. Vervollständige die folgenden Fragen, indem du das am besten in den Zusammenhang passende Hilfsverb verwendest (*can, must* oder *may*).

a) _____ I go swimming?

b) _____ Martin work late?

c) _____ you open the window?

d) _____ you help me push my car?

e) _____ Rachel stay at home, she isn't ill?

f) _____ I help you?

g) _____ Robert come to my party?

h) _____ Mark carry grandad's suitcase?

i) _____ you take a photo with my camera?

j) _____ we go to Aunty Freda's for lunch?

- Die Bedeutung von *have/has got to* ist ähnlich der von *must*. Es wird verwendet, wenn etwas notwendig oder verpflichtend ist, aber die Verpflichtung nicht vom Sprecher ausgeht, sondern allgemein ist und unter Umständen schon vorher bestanden hat.

  Beispiel: I've got to do my homework tonight.

  Bei der verneinten Aussage wird *not* nach *have/has* eingefügt.

  Beispiel: I haven't got to walk on the grass.

  In Aussagesätzen werden normalerweise die Kurzformen verwendet: *I've got to ..., she's got to ...* usw. In verneinten Aussagesätzen werden gewöhnlich folgende Kurzformen verwendet: *I haven't got to ..., she hasn't got to ...* usw. Statt *have/has got to* wird häufig *have/has to* verwendet, ohne dass sich die Bedeutung ändert.

  In Fragen mit *have/has got to* steht das Subjekt des Satzes zwischen *have* und *got to*.

  Beispiel: Have they got to wash up?

... rund ums Verb: Hilfsverben

28. Mr und Mrs Wells haben gestern ihren Kindern gesagt, was sie heute tun müssen. Mr Wells hat mit Polly gesprochen und Mrs Wells mit Chris. Manchmal waren beide Kinder angesprochen. Schreibe in vollständigen Sätzen auf, was zu Polly, zu Chris oder zu beiden gesagt wurde.

a) Polly has got to meet her mother at 4.00 p.m.
b) ___
c) ___
d) ___
e) ___
f) ___
g) ___
h) ___
i) ___
j) ___

... rund ums Verb: Hilfsverben

29. Benutze deine Antworten aus Übung 28, um passende Fragen zu bilden.

a) _Has Polly got to meet her mother at 4.00 p.m.?_

b) _____

c) _____

d) _____

e) _____

f) _____

g) _____

h) _____

i) _____

j) _____

30. Übersetze die folgenden Sätze.

a) Ich muss dieses Buch für die Schule lesen.

_____

b) Sie dürfen nicht nach Belfast zu fliegen.

_____

c) Müssen wir mit dem Zug fahren?

_____

d) Musst du deine Postkarten schreiben?

_____

11 Gerundium als Subjekt

Wann verwendest du ein Gerundium?

Das **Gerundium** (*gerund*) kannst du niemals als Prädikat eines Satzes benutzen, weil es – genau wie Infinitiv und Partizip – eine **infinite Verbform** ist. Das Gerundium gleicht aber stark dem **Nomen,** was du z. B. daran sehen kannst, dass es **Subjekt** eines Satzes sein kann.
Beispiel: Driving is fun.

Wie bildest du das Gerundium?

watch →	watching	Im Normalfall: Verb + -*ing*. Deshalb wird das *gerund* auch oft als 'ing-Form des Verbs' bezeichnet.
run →	running	Wenn der vorausgehende Vokal kurz ist: Verdoppelung des Konsonanten
drive →	driving	Wenn das Verb mit einem -*e* endet, so fällt dieses weg.
tie →	tying	Aus -*ie* am Ende des Verbs wird -*y*.

1. Bilde das Gerundium von folgenden Verben.

   a) close _____ b) hop _____

   c) hope _____ d) stay _____

   e) cry _____ f) lie _____

   g) cut _____ h) stand _____

   i) go _____ j) run _____

   k) sit _____ l) make _____

   m) play _____ n) ask _____

... rund um den Satz: Gerundium als Subjekt

2. Bilde zu den folgenden Bildern passende Sätze.

a)  _____ is fun.

b)  _____ is Henry's hobby.

c)  _____ is exciting.

d)  _____ is nice.

e) 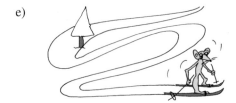 _____ is wonderful.

... rund um den Satz: Gerundium als Subjekt

Als Subjekt des Satzes kannst du das Gerundium auch mit einem Objekt verbinden. Dann sind das Gerundium und das Objekt Subjekt des ganzen Satzes.

Beispiel: Playing tennis is difficult.

3. Vervollständige die folgenden Sätze, indem du eine *ing*-Form des Verbs zusammen mit einem Objekt verwendest. Hier sind die Verben, die du für diese Übung benötigst: *find / buy / tie / open / visit / watch / clean / phone*

   a) _____ is fantastic.

   b) _____ is Gary's job.

   c) _____ is difficult.

   d) _____ is easy.
   (shoelace = 'Schnürsenkel')

... rund um den Satz: Gerundium als Subjekt

e) _____ is expensive.

f) _____ doesn't always make Annabel happy.

g) _____ isn't easy.

h) _____ isn't fun.

4. Übersetze die folgenden Sätze.

a) Bücher zu schreiben ist schwierig.

_____

b) Joggen macht Spaß.

_____

c) Basketballspielen ist Lindas Hobby.

_____

158

12 Imperativ

> **Wann und wie verwendest du den Imperativ?**
> Du benutzt Imperative, wenn du Befehle oder Anweisungen geben möchtest. Die Form des Imperativs gleicht der des Infinitivs. Allerdings entfällt beim Imperativ das *to*. Im Englischen gibt es keinen Unterschied zwischen dem Imperativ im Singular und dem Imperativ im Plural.
> *Beispiele:* "Where is my jacket?" – "<u>Look</u> upstairs."
> We can see them running away. – "<u>Stop</u> them!"

1. Während eines Landschulheim-Aufenthaltes der 5. Klasse machte Jessica bei vielen Aktivitäten mit. Ihre Freunde riefen ihr jeweils zu, was sie als nächstes tun sollte. Finde für jede Zeichnung den passenden Imperativ aus der Liste und schreibe ihn in die Sprechblase: *Climb over it! / Turn left! / Go under it! / Kick it! / Look this way! / Stop now!*

... rund um den Satz: Imperativ

2. Welche Imperative können mit dem Gegenstand im Kreis und den Tätigkeiten in den Pfeilen gebraucht werden? Die deutschen Ausdrücke sollen dir helfen.

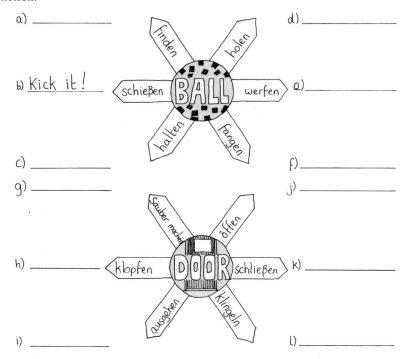

a) _____

b) Kick it! _____

c) _____

d) _____

e) _____

f) _____

g) _____

h) _____

i) _____

j) _____

k) _____

l) _____

Du gebrauchst den **verneinten Imperativ,** wenn du jemandem sagen möchtest, was er nicht tun soll, wenn du jemanden vor etwas warnen oder aber ihm einen Rat geben willst. Du bildest verneinte Imperative mit *don't* + Infinitiv ohne *to*.

Beispiele: Don't walk on the grass!   (Befehl)
             Don't go across the road, Susan!   (Warnung)
             Don't phone me tomorrow, I'm in London.   (Rat)

3. Während seiner Ferien sah Jim einige merkwürdige Verbotsschilder. Schreibe einen passenden verneinten Imperativ zu jedem Schild.

a) _____
b) _____
c) _____
d) _____
e) _____
f) _____
g) _____
h) _____
i) _____
j) _____

... rund um den Satz: Imperativ

4. Schreibe passende verneinte Imperative (Ratschläge) zu den folgenden Situationen. Die Verben, die du für deine Sätze brauchst, stehen in Klammern.

a) A green door is not nice. (paint)
   Don't paint the door green.

b) The library is not open. (go)

c) You need an umbrella. (forget)

d) Grandma is ill today. (visit)

e) The bank is open until 5 o'clock. (run)

f) The water is very cold. (swim)

g) That is a big tree. (climb)

5. Mrs Grooms Kinder sind im Garten und sind sehr ungezogen. Übersetze, was die Mutter zu ihren Kindern sagt.

a) Klettert nicht auf die Bäume!
b) Steh' nicht auf den Blumen!
c) Werft keine Steine!
d) Kämpft nicht!

a) _____
b) _____
c) _____
d) _____

13 Fragen mit Fragewörtern

Fragen kannst du mit oder ohne Fragewörter bilden. Wie du Fragen ohne Fragewörter bilden kannst, siehst du z. B. auf den Seiten 106, 115 und 139.

Rund um *what*

Wann und wie gebrauchst du das Fragewort *what*?
- Du gebrauchst *what* ('was'), um Fragen über den **Besitz** einer Sache zu stellen. Es wird zusammen mit *has/have got* benutzt.
  Beispiele: What have Julia and Peter got?
  What has she got in her bag?
- Du kannst *what* ('was') aber auch benutzen, um **nach Dingen zu fragen, die gerade passieren.**
  Beispiel: What is Robert doing?

1. Bilde anhand der Abbildungen und der vorgegebenen Antworten die passenden Fragen.

163

... rund um den Satz: Fragen mit Fragewörtern

a) Frage: _What is on the chair?_
   Antwort: A shoe is on the chair.
b) Frage: _____
   Antwort: Lucy and Rebecca have got bottles in the box.
c) Frage: _____
   Antwort: Ann has got an apple.
d) Frage: _____
   Antwort: John and Mike are watching television.
e) Frage: _____
   Antwort: The dog's name is Rover.
f) Frage: _____
   Antwort: The cats are drinking milk.
g) Frage: _____
   Antwort: A book is on the table.
h) Frage: _____
   Antwort: Tom is carrying a picture.
i) Frage: _____
   Antwort: John has got an ice-cream.
j) Frage: _____
   Antwort: A ball is under the table.
k) Frage: _____
   Antwort: Rebecca is wearing a baseball hat.

2. Übersetze die folgenden Sätze.

   a) Was haben die Hunde?
   _____

   b) Was trägt Jane (gerade)?
   _____

   c) Was hat Tim in der (= seiner) Hand?
   _____

... rund um den Satz: Fragen mit Fragewörtern

Rund um *how (how old, how many, how much)*

Wann und wie gebrauchst du *how* und seine Zusammensetzungen?

how	wie	*Beispiel:* How are you?
how old	wie alt	*Beispiel:* How old is Ian?
how many	wie viele	*Beispiel:* How many books are here?
how much	wie viel	*Beispiel:* How much water have you got?

- *how many* gebrauchst du immer bei **zählbaren Gegenständen**. Das nachfolgende Nomen steht immer im Plural.
  Beispiel: How many dogs are there? – There are six dogs.

- *how much* benutzt du immer bei **nicht zählbaren Dingen**, z. B. Wasser oder Benzin. Diese unzählbaren Nomen haben keine Pluralform.
  Beispiel: How much money have you got?

3. Vervollständige die folgenden Fragen.

   a) _____ petrol have you got?

   b) _____ is petrol?

   c) _____ biscuits are on the table?

   d) _____ are you?

   e) _____ money has Georgina got?

   f) _____ children are in the school?

   g) _____ chocolate has Luke got?

   h) _____ men and women are on the bus?

4. Übersetze die folgenden Sätze.

   a) Wie alt ist Kathy?
   _____

   b) Wie viel Limonade hat Henry?
   _____

Rund um *where*

Wann und wie gebrauchst du das Fragewort *where*?

Du verwendest *where,* wenn du wissen möchtest, **wo** sich eine Person oder eine Sache befindet, oder wenn du wissen möchtest, **woher** jemand kommt.

Beispiele: Where are my socks?
Where is Julia from?

5. Vervollständige die folgenden Fragen. Beantworte dann die Fragen mithilfe der Bilder.

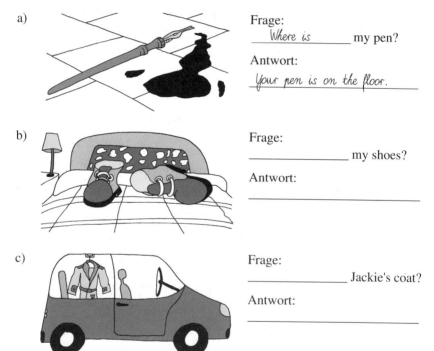

a) Frage:
_____Where is_____ my pen?
Antwort:
Your pen is on the floor.

b) Frage:
_____ my shoes?
Antwort:
_____

c) Frage:
_____ Jackie's coat?
Antwort:
_____

... rund um den Satz: Fragen mit Fragewörtern

d) Frage:
_____ Mike?
Antwort:
_____

e) Frage:
_____ the dog and the cat?
Antwort:
_____

f) Frage:
_____ Bill from?
Antwort:
_____

g) Frage:
_____ in Great Britain _____ they _____?
Antwort:
_____

h) Frage:
_____ the camera?
Antwort:
_____

... rund um den Satz: Fragen mit Fragewörtern

Rund um *who*

Wann und wie gebrauchst du das Fragewort *who*?
Du verwendest *who* ('wer'), wenn du wissen willst, **wer** etwas tut. *who* ist in Fragen dieser Art Subjekt des Fragesatzes. *who* bezieht sich immer auf Personen.
Beispiel: Who is driving?

6. Vervollständige die folgenden Fragen. Beantworte dann die Fragen mithilfe der Bilder.

a) Frage:
_____ Steve's friend?
Antwort:

b) Frage:
_____ they?
Antwort:

c) Frage:
_____ playing football?
Antwort:

... rund um den Satz: Fragen mit Fragewörtern

d) Frage:
_____ talking?
Antwort:
_____

e) Frage:
_____ Kim and Barry visiting?
Antwort:
_____

f) Frage:
_____ in the café?
Antwort:
_____

g) Frage:
_____ Tina phoning?
Antwort:
_____

h) Frage:
_____ you meeting?
Antwort:
_____

... rund um den Satz: Fragen mit Fragewörtern

7. Gemischte Übung: Welches ist in den folgenden Fragen das richtige Fragewort: *how, how much, how many, how old, what, where* oder *who*?

a) _____ is the bus from?

b) _____ are Paula and John doing?

c) _____ is riding that bike over there?

d) _____ pens are in the box?

e) _____ have the cats got?

f) _____ is the bus?

g) _____ is Carol going?

h) _____ is visiting Glasgow next week?

i) _____ money have you got?

j) _____ is that man doing?

k) _____ has he got in his hand?

l) _____ are you next birthday?

m) _____ is in the shop?

n) _____ is at the door?

o) _____ water is in the bottle?

p) _____ are Susan's friends going?

8. Übersetze die folgenden Sätze.

a) Wer ist in der Garage?

_____

b) Wo sind die Fotografien?

_____

c) Wer sind Georges Freunde?

_____

d) Woher ist Janice?

_____

Rund um *whose*

Wann und wie gebrauchst du das Fragewort *whose*?
Du gebrauchst das Fragewort *whose*, wenn du wissen willst, **wem** etwas **gehört** (**wessen**).
Beispiel: "Whose coat is on the chair?" – "It's Joan's coat."

9. Mr Philips Schüler vergessen immer Sachen, wenn sie das Klassenzimmer verlassen. Schaue dir das Bild sorgfältig an und bilde dann die Fragen, die Mr Philips stellt. (Achte auch auf *this/that* und *these/those*.)

... rund um den Satz: Fragen mit Fragewörtern

a) Whose watch is this?
b) _____ coats _____?
c) _____?
d) _____?
e) _____ on the floor?
f) _____ on the chair?

10. *whose*, *who's* (*who is*) und *who's got* kann man leicht verwechseln. Vervollständige die folgenden Sätze, indem du den jeweils richtigen Ausdruck einsetzt.

   a) _____ at the door?
   b) _____ jacket is this?
   c) _____ grandparents live in America?
   d) _____ a pencil?
   e) _____ pencil is blue?
   f) _____ reading the book today?
   g) _____ book is it?
   h) _____ a book?
   i) _____ called Tina?
   j) _____ dog is Henry?
   k) _____ in the photograph?

   (Weitere Übungen zu *whose*, *who's* und *who's got* findest du auf Seite 185.)

11. Übersetze die folgenden Sätze.

   a) Wer hat ein neues Fahrrad?
   _____

   b) Wessen Auto ist neu?
   _____

... rund um den Satz: Fragen mit Fragewörtern

12. Gemischte Übung: Brum und Harger leben seit vielen Jahren auf dem Planeten Costalot. Heute kommen unerwartete Besucher an.

a) Kannst du ihre Unterhaltung vervollständigen, indem du die passenden Fragewörter einsetzt? *what, how (how old* usw.*), where, who, whose, why*

b) Kannst du herausfinden, was die amerikanischen Astronauten auf Costalot wollten? Schaue dir dazu sorgfältig den Comic an. Brum und Harger können dir auch bei der Rätselfrage helfen.
Was nahmen sie mit zur Erde zurück?

___ ___ ___ ___ ___ ___ ___ ___ ___ (s)

c) Wortbildung: Wie viele Wörter kannst du um **jeden** Buchstaben des Nahrungsmittels, das die Astronauten gefunden haben, herum bilden?
Jedes Wort einer Wortgruppe muss jeweils mit demselben Anfangsbuchstaben beginnen und jedes neue Wort muss einen Buchstaben länger sein als das vorherige.
Fange jeweils mit dem kürzesten Wort an. Du darfst keinen Plural benutzen (und auch kein Wörterbuch oder Schulbuch!).

Beispiel: **Buchstabe B**
be – bed – bell – bread – before – burglar – building – boyfriend – basketball

Rund um Fragewörter mit *do/does*

Wann und wie gebrauchst du Fragewörter mit *do/does*?
Wenn die Frage keine Form von *to be* und auch kein Hilfsverb enthält, musst du *do/does* mit dem **Vollverb und dem Fragewort** verwenden. Die Satzkonstruktion lautet dann: Fragewort + *do/does* + Subjekt + Verb + Objekt
Beispiel: <u>Where</u> <u>do</u> we <u>buy</u> shoes?

13. Mrs Nelson fährt ihren Mann nach London, weil sein Auto kaputt ist. Ihre Kinder Joey und Fiona sind den ganzen Tag auf sich gestellt. Kannst du aus den Antworten, die ihre Eltern geben, Joeys und Fionas Fragen erschließen?

   a) __Why do__ you drive dad to London?
      Because his car is in the garage.

   b) _____ we make breakfast?
      At 7.30 a.m.

   c) _____ I buy milk?
      At the supermarket.

   d) _____ bread cost?
      It costs £ 1.25.

   e) _____ we eat for lunch?
      There are pizzas in the fridge.

   f) _____ we cook the pizzas?
      The instructions are on the packet.

   g) _____ we have for dinner?
      You go to Jenny's!

   h) _____ Jenny live?
      Her address is on the table.

   i) _____ Jenny do?
      She works with me.

   j) _____ you leave London?
      At 10.00 p.m.

... rund um den Satz: Fragen mit Fragewörtern

14. **Gemischte Übung:** Lies den folgendne Text sorgfältig und vervollständige dann die Fragen mit einem Fragewort und einer Form von *to do*. Die Fragen stehen in der richtigen Reihenfolge.

    Ben comes from Lincoln. Today he has to go to Scotland to meet Julia. Julia works in Perth. Ben knows Julia because they went to school together. Ben and Julia are engineers. Ben leaves Lincoln at 4.00 a.m. he is going to meet Julia at Stirling because they are going to go to Glasgow. Last year they met at the same place. They go home on Friday. Ben has to go to Paris next week.

    a) _____ Ben come from?
    b) _____ he have to go to Scotland?
    c) _____ Julia work?
    d) _____ Ben know Julia?
    e) _____ Ben and Julia do?
    f) _____ Ben leave Lincoln?
    g) _____ Ben and Julia meet at Stirling?
    h) _____ they know where to meet?
    i) _____ they go home?
    j) _____ Ben have to go next week?

15. Übersetze die folgenden Sätze.

    a) Wo kauft Tony seine Kleidung?
    _____

    b) Warum sammelst du Briefmarken?
    _____

    c) Wie kommt Karen zur Schule?
    _____

Rund um *who* als Objekt

Wann und wie gebrauchst du das Fragewort *who* als Objekt?
who kann auch Objekt des Fragesatzes sein, aber in diesem Fall musst du zur Bildung der Frage eine Form von *do/does* oder ein Hilfsverb verwenden. *who* hat dann die Bedeutung von 'wen' oder 'wem'.

Beispiele: Who can I paint today? (wen)
Who does Mary visit? (wen)
Who must Peter write to? (wem)

16. Hier sind die Antworten zu einigen *who*-Fragen. Stelle die entsprechenden Fragen.

    a) _____
    Ann meets Dave at the station.

    b) _____
    Adam can visit Harry.

    c) _____
    We must telephone Mr Carter.

    d) _____
    They talk to Mrs Miller.

    e) _____
    She can play with Suzy.

    f) _____
    Colin must take his brother to the party.

17. Übersetze die folgenden Sätze.

    a) Wen muss ich anrufen?

    _____

    b) Mit wem spricht sie?

    _____

    c) Wem kann sie helfen?

    _____

* 18. **Gemischte Übung:** Frankensteins Monster: Dr. Josephine Frankenstein hat Professor Grim damit beauftragt, ihre neueste Schöpfung zusammenzusetzen. Aber der zerstreute Professor ist weggegangen, um ein Fußballspiel anzuschauen, und hat es seinen Gehilfen Sweeney, Hyde and Stitcher überlassen, die Pläne auszuführen.
Kannst du alle fehlenden Fragewörter mit den richtigen Formen der Hilfsverben, von *to be* und von *do/does* einsetzen?

HYDE: _____ we build Franky?
SWEENEY: _____ you ask me?
HYDE: Because you have got the plans.
SWEENEY: No, I haven't.
HYDE: _____ the plans then?
SWEENEY: The plans are with Professor Grim.
HYDE: _____ the Professor now?
SWEENEY: At the football match.
HYDE: Oh, wonderful!! We have to build Franky without a plan! OK then, let's start. _____ the head?
SWEENEY: _____ head do you want?
HYDE: The head in box number two. Next, _____ got the neck from box one?
STITCHER: Here it is. But _____ the arms and the body?
HYDE: The arms are in box six and the body is in box five, I think.
SWEENEY: _____ time have we got to build Franky?
HYDE: Until the football match ends!
STITCHER: OK, _____ I find his feet?
HYDE: Feet are in boxes three and four. Put the feet on the legs. The legs are in box nine.
SWEENEY: _____ hands do we use?
HYDE: Oh, hello Professor.
PROFESSOR: Hello Hyde.
HYDE: One question Professor. _____ Franky's hands?
PROFESSOR: I don't know, try box eight! _____ I always have to decide!

HYDE: Here he is Professor, meet Franky.
PROFESSOR: No! No! No! This isn't Franky! This is terrible! _____ I tell Dr Frankenstein?

Wenn du sehen willst, welchen schrecklichen Fehler die Arbeiter gemacht haben, setze die Teile des Körpers genauso zusammen, wie sie es getan haben.

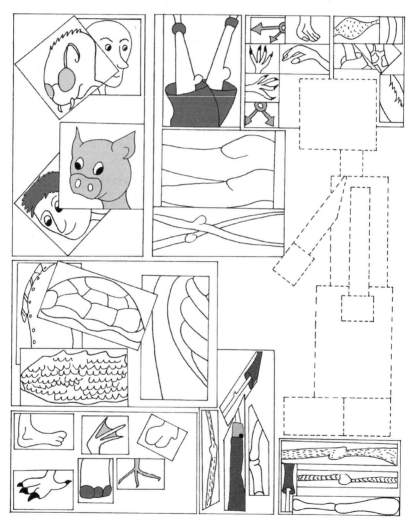

14 *there is-*, *there are*-Konstruktionen

Wann und wie verwendest du die *there is-*, *there are*-Konstruktionen?

there is-, *there are*-Konstruktionen verwendest du vor allem dann, wenn du anfängst, von einem neuen Thema zu sprechen. Die Folgesätze formulierst du in der Regel als ganz normale Aussagesätze. ***there is*** ist die **Singularform** und bezieht sich auf einen Gegenstand oder eine Person oder etwas Unzählbares, z. B. Wasser. ***there are*** ist die **Pluralform** und bezieht sich auf Dinge oder Personen im Plural.

Beispiele: There is a teacher.
There is water on the floor.
There are five bananas.

1. Sieh dir die folgenden Bilder an und schreibe dann zu jedem Bild einen Satz mit *there is* oder *there are*.

a) There are two doctors.
b) _____
c) _____
d) _____
e) _____
f) _____
g) _____
h) _____

2. Hier ist das Bild einer Straße, auf dem viel zu sehen ist. Schreibe Sätze über das, was du siehst, und benutze dabei die Ausdrücke, die in Klammern stehen.

a) *There is a bus stop in front of the clothes shop.*
(bus stop / clothes shop)

b) _____ in front of _____
(taxi / post office)

c) _____ in front of _____
(bicycle / bakery)

d) _____
(robber / bank)

e) _____
(policeman / taxi)

f) _____
(old man / shoe shop)

g) _____
(flower / window)

h) _____
(tree / bank)

i) _____
(bus / bookshop)

15 Homophone

Wörter, die ähnlich klingen aber eine **unterschiedliche Bedeutung** haben, nennt man **Homophone**. Pass immer gut auf, dass du solche gleich lautenden Ausdrücke nicht miteinander verwechselst. Im Folgenden sind ein paar Homophone aufgelistet. Sieh dir die folgenden Seiten gut an, dann wirst du sicherlich keine Schwierigkeiten mit den Homophonen haben.

Rund um *its* und *it's*

- *its*   sein / ihr
  Beispiel: The tree is losing <u>its</u> leaves.
  Der Baum verliert <u>seine</u> Blätter.

- *it's (= it is)*   es ist
  Beispiel: Today, <u>it's</u> snowing.
  Heute <u>schneit es</u>.

- *it's got (= it has got)*   es hat
  Beispiel: The house is new. <u>It's got</u> a large garden.
  Das Haus ist neu. <u>Es hat</u> einen großen Garten.

1. Vervollständige die folgenden kurzen Texte, indem du, wo es nötig ist, den Apostroph ergänzt, um zwischen *its* und *it's* zu unterscheiden.

   a)  Today, its a holiday.
   Diana is driving her car.
   Its an old car.
   Its colour is black.

Anhang: Homophone

b)

That dog is big.
I think its a nice dog but I never see it with its owner.

c)

This bag is old.
Its got a hole in it.
Its contents always fall out onto the floor.
(contents = Inhalt)

d)

Its an old hotel.
Its windows are new but its doors are old.
Its near the sea but its got a swimming pool in its garden.

e)

The farm is in Yorkshire.
Its a large farm.
Its got cows, pigs and sheep.
Today, its its open day. Many people visit the farm and see its animals and its tractors.
Its an interesting place to visit.
(open day = 'Tag der offenen Tür')

Rund um *their* und *there*

- **their** — ihr
  Beispiel: It is their car.
  Es ist ihr Auto. (2. Person Plural)

- **there** — da / dort
  Beispiel: Pamela buys her clothes there.
  Pamela kauft sich dort ihre Kleider.

- **there is/are** — es gibt
  Beispiel: There are nice shops in London.
  Es gibt in London schöne Geschäfte.

- **over there** — dort hinüber / dort drüben
  Beispiel: Over there is a policeman.
  Dort drüben ist ein Polizist.

2. Vervollständige die folgenden Sätze mit *there (there, there is/are* oder *over there)* oder *their*.

a) _____ garden is nice.

b) _____ a large park in London.

c) _____ many people _____ .

d) _____ is the swimming pool.

e) Mr and Mrs Jackson always go to Spain for _____ holidays.

f) Over _____ , _____ an old plane.

g) Is that _____ boat, _____ ?

h) That is not _____ house. _____ house is the blue house, _____ .

i) _____ two coats here. Are they _____ coats?

j) Heather and Karen often go to Calais for the day. _____ many shops _____ . Heather and Karen also like to buy _____ clothes _____ and not in England.

183

Anhang: Homophone

Rund um *your* und *you're*

- ***your***   dein / euer / ihr
  Beispiel: Here is y<u>our</u> pencil.
  Hier ist <u>dein</u> Stift

- ***you're*** (= *you are*)   du bist / Sie sind / ihr seid
  Beispiel: Paula thinks y<u>ou're</u> Martin.
  Paula denkt <u>du bist</u> Martin.

3. Vervollständige die folgenden Sätze mit *your* oder *you're*.

   a) Is that _____ car?
   b) _____ very tall.
   c) _____ in France now.
   d) _____ coats are here.
   e) "Jenny, _____ friend is waiting for you and _____ late."
   f) "_____ not to read _____ book in bed."
   g) This isn't _____ photograph.
   h) Are you listening to _____ radio today?
   i) Today, it's _____ birthday. _____ 12 years old.
   j) _____ very lucky, you can see _____ house from here.
   k) _____ a good footballer.
   l) Have you got _____ bag?
   m) _____ mother thinks _____ at school!
   n) _____ Tony and _____ sister is Tracey.
   o) My friend likes _____ coat.
   p) Have you all got _____ sandwiches?
   q) _____ umbrella is on _____ desk.

Rund um *whose, who's* und *who's got*

- ***whose***   wem gehört / wessen
  Beispiel: <u>Whose</u> gloves are on the table?
  <u>Wessen</u> Handschuhe sind auf dem Tisch?

- ***who's*** *(who is)*   wer ist
  Beispiel: <u>Who's</u> playing tennis?
  <u>Wer</u> spielt Tennis?

- ***who's got*** *(who has got)*   wer hat
  Beispiel: <u>Who's got</u> a computer?
  <u>Wer hat</u> einen Computer?

4. Vervollständige die folgenden Sätze mit *whose*, *who's* oder *who's got*.

a)    _____ a big house?

b)   _____ house is big ?

c)    _____ riding that bicycle?

Anhang: Homophone

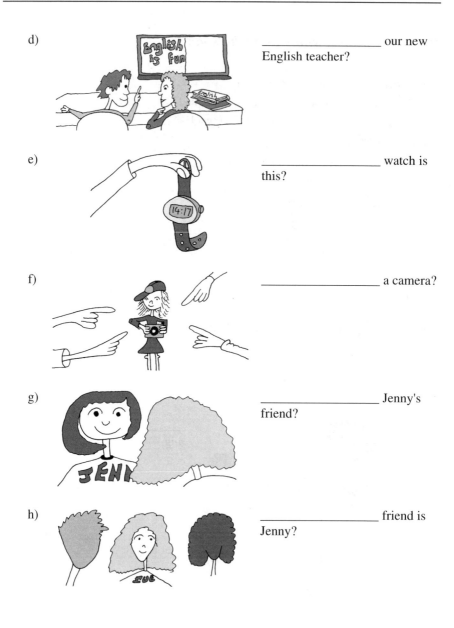

d) _____ our new English teacher?

e) _____ watch is this?

f) _____ a camera?

g) _____ Jenny's friend?

h) _____ friend is Jenny?

Anhang: Homophone

i)  _____ my pencil?

j) _____ Rupert phoning?

✱ 5. Es ist manchmal schwieriger, den Unterschied zwischen gleichlautenden Ausdrücken herauszufinden, wenn sie gesprochen werden, als wenn sie geschrieben werden. Deshalb versuche, diese Übung auf eine der folgenden Weisen zu machen.
- Bitte jemanden, die folgenden Texte langsam vorzulesen. Schreibe die ähnlich klingenden Wörter in der Reihenfolge auf, in der sie vorgelesen werden, und kontrolliere dann selbst, ob du sie richtig geschrieben hast.
- Du kannst auch den Text selbst laut lesen und auf eine Cassette aufnehmen. Höre ihn dir dann ein paar Tage später an und überprüfe, ob du die ähnlich klingenden Wörter richtig schreiben kannst.

a) *their* oder *there*

Ann and Michael are on holiday in Richmond. <u>Their</u> friends live <u>there</u>. <u>There</u> are many things to see in the town. Over <u>there</u> is a castle and <u>there</u> is a nice market place. Ann and Michael usually buy <u>their</u> cheese at that shop over <u>there</u>. <u>There</u> is also a river and a theatre in Richmond. The theatre is <u>their</u> favourite theatre. Ann and Michael often visit <u>their</u> friends because Richmond is a nice town.

Anhang: Homophone

b) *its* oder *it's*

Today, Janet and Tim are visiting Whitby. It's a small town next to the sea. It's famous for its 199 steps to its abbey. It's also famous for its fresh fish and a man called Captain Cook. It's a nice town and it's got lots of things to see. It's a good place for a holiday.

famous = berühmt
step = Stufe
abbey = Abtei

c) *your* oder *you're*

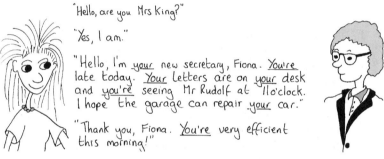

"Hello, are you Mrs King?"

"Yes, I am."

"Hello, I'm your new secretary, Fiona. You're late today. Your letters are on your desk and you're seeing Mr Rudolf at 11 o'clock. I hope the garage can repair your car."

"Thank you, Fiona. You're very efficient this morning!"

d) *whose* oder *who's*

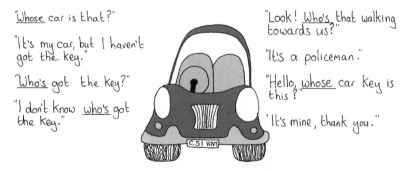

"Whose car is that?"

"It's my car, but I haven't got the key."

"Who's got the key?"

"I don't know who's got the key."

"Look! Who's that walking towards us?"

"It's a policeman."

"Hello, whose car key is this?"

"It's mine, thank you."

e) **Zusätzliche Übung:** Falls du noch mehr üben möchtest, bitte jemanden, dir die Lösungen der Übungen 1 bis 3 vorzulesen, oder nimm sie selbst auf Cassette auf. Dann finde die gleich lautenden Wörter heraus.

16 Schwierige Wörter, die wir in diesem Buch benutzen

Nicht alle in diesem Buch verwendeten Wörter stehen in der Vokabelliste, z. B. Wochen- und Monatsnamen, Zahlen, Personalpronomen, *a, an, the, to be* solltest du kennen, bzw. du kannst sie im Vokabelverzeichnis deines Englischbuches nachschlagen.

16.1 Englisch – Deutsch

abbey	–	Abtei	awake	– wach
accident	–	Unfall	away	– weg
across	–	über		
address	–	Adresse	baby	– Baby
after	–	nach	bag	– Tasche
afternoon	–	Nachmittag	baker	– Bäcker
again	–	nochmals/wieder	bakery	– Bäckerei
airport	–	Flughafen	ball	– Ball
also	–	auch	banana	– Banane
always	–	immer	bank	– Bank
America	–	Amerika	(to) bark	– bellen
American	–	amerikanisch/	baseball	– Baseball
		Amerikaner(in)	basketball team	– Basketballmannschaft
and	–	und	(to) be	– sein
animal	–	Tier	(to) be going to	– die Absicht haben zu/
another	–	noch einer/weiterer/		werden
		anderer	beautiful	– schön
answer	–	Antwort	because	– weil
apple	–	Apfel	bed	– Bett
arm	–	Arm	bedroom	– Schlafzimmer
arrival	–	Ankunft	before	– vor
(to) arrive	–	ankommen	(to) begin	– beginnen
(to) ask	–	fragen	behind	– hinter
assistant	–	Assistent	bell	– Klingel
astronaut	–	Astronaut(in)	belt	– Gürtel
Australia	–	Australien	bicycle (bike)	– Fahrrad
aunt/aunty	–	Tante	big	– groß

189

Anhang: Schwierige Wörter, die wir in diesem Buch benutzen

bird	–	Vogel	(to) cheat	– schwindeln
birthday	–	Geburtstag	cheese	– Käse
biscuit	–	Keks	child (children)	– Kind (Kinder)
black	–	schwarz	chips	– Pommes Frittes
blue	–	blau	chocolate	– Schokolade
boat	–	Boot	Christmas	– Weihnachten
body	–	Körper	church	– Kirche
bonfire	–	Freudenfeuer	cinema	– Kino
Bonfire Night	–	(5. November)	circle	– Kreis
book	–	Buch	circus	– Zirkus
bookshelves	–	Bücherregale	city	– Großstadt
boring	–	langweilig	class	– Klasse
born	–	geboren	(to) clean	– putzen/sauber machen
bottle	–	Flasche	(to) climb	– klettern
box	–	Karton	clock	– Uhr
Boxing Day	–	2. Weihnachtsfeiertag	(to) close	– schließen
boy	–	Junge	clothes	– Kleidung
boyfriend	–	Freund	clown	– Clown
bread	–	Brot	clue	– Anhaltspunkt/Schlüssel
breakfast	–	Frühstück	coat	– Mantel
bridge	–	Brücke	coconut	– Kokosnuss
(to) bring	–	bringen	cold	– kalt
brother	–	Bruder	(to) collect	– sammeln
brush	–	Bürste	colour	– Farbe
(to) build	–	bauen	(to) come	– kommen
building	–	Bau/Gebäude	(to) come from	– kommen aus ...
burglar	–	Einbrecher	comic	– Comic(heft)
burglary	–	Einbruch	computer	– Computer
bus	–	Bus	concert	– Konzert
bus stop	–	Bushaltestelle	(to) cook	– kochen
but	–	aber	(a) cook	– Koch/Köchin
(to) buy	–	kaufen	cool	– kühl
by	–	von	contents	– Inhalt
			corner	– Ecke
café	–	Café	(to) cost	– kosten
cake	–	Kuchen	country	– Land
(to be) called	–	heißen	course	– Kurs
camel	–	Kamel	cousin	– Cousin(e)
camera	–	Kamera	cow	– Kuh
can	–	können	(to) cry	– weinen
car	–	Auto	crocodile	– Krokodil
car park	–	Parkplatz	(to) cross	– überqueren
(to) carry	–	tragen	(a) crossing	– Kreuzung
cassette	–	Kassette	cup	– Tasse
castle	–	Burg	cupboard	– Schrank
cat	–	Katze	(to) cut	– schneiden
(to) catch	–	fangen	(to) cycle	– Rad fahren
(to) catch a train	–	einen Zug erreichen		
cathedral	–	Dom/Kathedrale	dad/Dad	– Vati
cave	–	Höhle	(to) dance	– tanzen
CD	–	CD	dancer	– Tänzer(in)
chair	–	Stuhl	daughter	– Tochter
(to) change	–	verändern	day	– Tag
(to) chat	–	sich unterhalten	Dear ...	– Liebe/r, Sehr geehrte/r
cheap	–	billig	(to) decide	– sich entscheiden

190

Anhang: Schwierige Wörter, die wir in diesem Buch benutzen

deer	– Hirsch	(to) fish	– angeln
(to) depart	– abfahren	flat tyre	– platter Reifen
departure	– Abflug	floor	– Fußboden/Stockwerk
desk	– Schreibtisch	flower	– Blume
(to) do	– machen	(to) fly	– fliegen
difficult	– schwer/schwierig	food	– Futter/Lebensmittel
dinner	– Essen/Hauptmahlzeit	foot (feet)	– Fuß (Füße)
doctor	– Arzt/Ärztin	football	– Fußball
dodgem car	– Autoscooter	football match	– Fußballspiel
dog	– Hund	football team	– Fußballmannschaft
door	– Tür	footballer	– Fußballspieler
(to) draw	– zeichnen	for	– für
dress	– Kleid	forest	– Wald
(to) drink	– trinken	(to) forget	– vergessen
drink	– Getränk	fox	– Fuchs
(to) drive	– fahren	France	– Frankreich
driver	– Fahrer	French	– französisch
(to) dry	– trocknen	fresh	– frisch
		fridge	– Kühlschrank
(the) Earth	– (die) Erde	friend	– Freund
early	– früh	frog	– Frosch
ear	– Ohr	from	– von/aus
easy	– leicht	fun	– Spaß
(to) eat	– essen		
efficient	– tüchtig	games	– Spiele
egg	– Ei	garage	– Garage
elephant	– Elefant	garden	– Garten
(to) end	– (be)enden	gate	– Tor
(at the) end of	– am Ende von ...	German	– deutsch/Deutsche(r)
engineer	– Ingenieur	Germany	– Deutschland
English	– englisch/hier: Engländer(in)	(to) get	– bekommen
entrance	– Eingang	(to) get in	– einsteigen
evening	– Abend	(to) get off	– aussteigen
every	– jeder/-e/-es	ghost train	– Geisterbahn
exciting	– spannend	giraffe	– Giraffe
expensive	– teuer	girl	– Mädchen
eye	– Auge	(to) give	– geben
		glass	– Glas
(a) fair	– Kirmes/Volksfest	gloves	– Handschuhe
fair ride (rides)	– Fahrt (auf dem Volksfest)	gold	– Gold
		golf	– Golf
family	– Familie	(to) go	– gehen
famous	– berühmt	(to) go home	– nach Hause gehen
fantastic	– phantastisch	good	– gut
farm	– Bauernhof	grandad	– Opa
fast	– schnell	grandfather	– Großvater
father	– Vater	grandma	– Oma
favourite	– Lieblings...	grandmother	– Großmutter
fax	– Fax	grandparents	– Großeltern
(to) feed	– füttern	grass	– Gras
(to) fetch	– holen	green	– grün
(to) fight	– kämpfen	Greenland	– Grönland
(to) find	– finden	guards	– Wachen
first	– erster/-e/-es	Guy Fawkes Night	– (5. November)
fish	– Fisch		

Anhang: Schwierige Wörter, die wir in diesem Buch benutzen

hair	–	Haar/Haare
Halloween	–	(31. Oktober)
hand	–	Hand
happy	–	glücklich
harbour	–	Hafen
has/have (got)	–	haben/besitzen
hat	–	Mütze/Hut
(to) have	–	haben
head	–	Kopf
(to) hear	–	hören
hedgehog	–	Igel
helicopter	–	Hubschrauber
(to) help	–	helfen
(to) help down	–	herunterhelfen
here	–	hier
high	–	hoch
(to) hit	–	treffen
hobby	–	Hobby
(to) hold	–	halten
hole	–	Loch
holiday	–	Urlaub/Ferien
home	–	zu Hause
homework	–	Hausaufgaben
(to) hop	–	hüpfen
(to) hope	–	hoffen
horse	–	Pferd
horserider	–	Reiter
hotel	–	Hotel
house	–	Haus
how	–	wie
how many	–	wie viele
how much	–	wie viel
ice-cream	–	Eis
idea	–	Idee
ill	–	krank
in	–	in
in front of	–	vor
India	–	Indien
in the middle (of)	–	in der Mitte
inside	–	innen
instruction	–	Anweisung
interesting	–	interessant
into	–	in/hinein
Ireland	–	Irland
island	–	Insel
jacket	–	Jacke
(to) jog	–	joggen
(to) jump	–	springen
junction	–	Kreuzung
kangaroo	–	Känguru
key	–	Schlüssel
(to) kick	–	treten
kilt	–	Kilt
king	–	König
kitchen	–	Küche
kite	–	Drache
(to) knock at	–	klopfen an ...
(to) know	–	wissen/kennen
lake	–	der See
lamp	–	Lampe
large	–	groß
(to be) late	–	zu spät kommen
Latin	–	Latein
(to) learn	–	lernen
leaves (leaf)	–	Blätter (Blatt)
(to) leave	–	abfliegen/(ver)lassen
left	–	links
leg	–	Bein
lemonade	–	Limonade
let's	–	lass/lasst uns
letter	–	Brief
level crossing	–	Bahnübergang
library	–	Bücherei
(to) lie	–	liegen
(a) light	–	Licht/Lampe
lighthouse	–	Leuchtturm
(to) like	–	mögen/gefallen
(to) listen	–	(zu)hören
little	–	klein/wenig
(to) live	–	wohnen/leben
(to) lock	–	abschließen
long	–	lang
(a) long way	–	weit
(to) look	–	sehen/gucken
(to) look after	–	sich kümmern um/sorgen für
(to) look cold	–	kalt aussehen
(to) lose	–	verlieren
(a) lot of	–	viel/viele
lots of	–	viel/viele
loud	–	laut
to be lucky	–	Glück haben
lunch	–	Mittagessen
lunchtime	–	Mittagszeit
made of	–	gemacht aus
main road	–	Hauptstraße
(to) make	–	machen
(to) make happy	–	glücklich machen
man	–	Mann
many	–	viele
map	–	Karte
market	–	Markt
market place	–	Marktplatz
may	–	dürfen

Anhang: Schwierige Wörter, die wir in diesem Buch benutzen

(to) meet	–	treffen	onto	–	auf (mit Akk.)
(to) mend	–	reparieren	on the left	–	auf der linken Seite
metre	–	Meter	on the right	–	auf der rechten Seite
milk	–	Milch	on top of	–	oben/auf
minute	–	Minute	open	–	offen
mirror	–	Spiegel	(to) open	–	öffnen
more	–	mehr	open day	–	Tag der offenen Tür
money	–	Geld	opposite	–	gegenüber
monkey	–	Affe	or	–	oder
monster	–	Monster	(an) orange	–	Orange/Apfelsine
month	–	Monat	(the) other	–	der, die, das andere ...
morning	–	Morgen	outside	–	außerhalb
mother	–	Mutter	over	–	über
motorbike	–	Motorrad	over there	–	dort hinüber/dort drüben
motorway	–	Autobahn	owner	–	Besitzer
mountain	–	Berg			
mountain bike	–	Mountainbike	packet	–	Schachtel/Packung
mouse	–	Maus	(a) painting	–	Bild/Gemälde
mouth	–	Mund	(to) paint	–	malen
(to) move	–	umziehen	(a) pair of		
music	–	Musik	glasses	–	Brille
musician	–	Musiker	parents	–	Eltern
must	–	müssen	(a) park	–	Park
museum	–	Museum	(to) park	–	parken
			party	–	Party
name	–	Name	pen	–	Füller
near	–	nahe/in der Nähe von	pencil	–	Bleistift
neck	–	Hals	people	–	Leute/Menschen
(to) need	–	brauchen/benötigen	perhaps	–	vielleicht
neighbour	–	Nachbar	pet	–	Haustier
never	–	nie	petrol	–	Benzin
new	–	neu	(to) phone	–	anrufen
New Year's Eve	–	Silvester	photo(graph)	–	Foto
newspaper	–	Zeitung	(to take) photos	–	Fotos machen
next	–	nächster/nächste/	pier	–	Pier
		nächstes	pig	–	Schwein
next door to	–	nebenan/neben	pilot	–	Pilot
next time	–	nächstes Mal	place	–	Ort
next to	–	neben	plane	–	Flugzeug
nice	–	schön/nett	plan	–	Plan
night	–	Nacht	(to) plan	–	planen
noise	–	Lärm	plant	–	Pflanze
no problem	–	kein Problem	platform	–	Bahnsteig/Gleis
nose	–	Nase	(to) play	–	spielen
not	–	nicht	please	–	bitte
now	–	jetzt	pocket	–	Tasche
number	–	Zahl/Nummer	police car	–	Polizeiauto
			policeman	–	Polizist
of	–	von	policewoman	–	Polizistin
of course	–	natürlich	pop concert	–	Popkonzert
office	–	Büro	pop group	–	Popgruppe
often	–	oft	postcard	–	Postkarte
old	–	alt	post office	–	Post(amt)
on	–	auf/an (mit Dativ)	postman	–	Briefträger
only	–	nur	potato	–	Kartoffel

193

Anhang: Schwierige Wörter, die wir in diesem Buch benutzen

(to) prefer	–	vorziehen
present	–	Geschenk
pretty	–	hübsch
prince	–	Prinz
princess	–	Prinzessin
(to) push	–	schieben
(to) put	–	setzen/stellen/legen
pyramid	–	Pyramide
queen	–	Königin
(a) question	–	Frage
(to be) quiet	–	leise/ruhig (sein)
radiator	–	Heizkörper
radio	–	Radio
railway	–	Eisenbahn
(to) rain	–	regnen
(to) read	–	lesen
ready	–	fertig
red	–	rot
(to) repair	–	reparieren
restaurant	–	Restaurant
rich	–	reich
(to) ride	–	fahren/reiten
right	–	rechts
(to) ring	–	klingeln
river	–	Fluss
road	–	Straße
robber	–	Räuber
rocket	–	Rakete
roof	–	Dach
room	–	Zimmer
round	–	rund/herum
roundabout	–	Kreisverkehr
(to) run	–	laufen/rennen
(to) sail	–	segeln
same place	–	dieselbe Stelle
sandals	–	Sandalen
sandwich	–	Butterbrot
sauna	–	Sauna
scarf	–	Schal
school	–	Schule
schoolchildren	–	Schulkinder
Scotland	–	Schottland
Scottish	–	schottisch/Schotten
sea	–	Meer
sea bird	–	Seevogel
sea lion	–	Seelöwe
(to) see	–	sehen
secretary	–	Sekretär(in)
(to) sell	–	verkaufen
(to) send	–	schicken
sheep	–	Schaf
shelf (shelves)	–	Regal
shirt	–	Hemd
shoe	–	Schuh
shoelace	–	Schnürsenkel
shop	–	Laden
shop assistant	–	Verkäufer(in)
(to go) shopping	–	einkaufen gehen
short	–	kurz
shorts	–	Shorts
(to) shut	–	schließen
(to) sing	–	singen
singer	–	Sänger(in)
sister	–	Schwester
(to) sit	–	sitzen
(to go) skateboarding	–	Skateboard fahren
(to) ski	–	Ski laufen
(to) sleep	–	schlafen
small	–	klein
snail	–	Schnecke
snake	–	Schlange
snow	–	Schnee
(to) snow	–	schneien
so	–	so
socks	–	Socken
sometimes	–	manchmal
song	–	Lied
soon	–	bald
(to be) sorry	–	Entschuldigung
south	–	südlich/Süden
(to) speak	–	sprechen
spider	–	Spinne
sports centre	–	Sportzentrum
squash	–	Squash
stamp	–	Briefmarke
(to) stand	–	stehen
(to) start	–	beginnen
start	–	Anfang
station	–	Bahnhof
(to) stay	–	vorübergehend wohnen
steam train	–	Dampfeisenbahn
step	–	Stufe
stool	–	Hocker
stone	–	Stein
(to) stop	–	anhalten
story	–	Geschichte
straight on	–	geradeaus
street	–	Straße
stripe	–	Streifen
suitcase	–	Koffer
summer	–	Sommer
sun	–	Sonne
sunglasses	–	Sonnebrille
sunshine	–	Sonnenschein
supermarket	–	Supermarkt
(to) swim	–	schwimmen

Anhang: Schwierige Wörter, die wir in diesem Buch benutzen

swimming	–	Schwimmen
swimming course	–	Schwimmunterricht
swimming pool	–	Schwimmbad
(to) switch on	–	einschalten
table	–	Tisch
(to) take	–	nehmen (jdn. mitnehmen)
(to) talk	–	sprechen
tall	–	groß
taxi	–	Taxi
tea	–	Tee
teacher	–	Lehrer(in)
telephone	–	Telefon
telephone box	–	Telefonzelle
television	–	Fernsehen
(to) tell	–	erzählen
tennis	–	Tennis
tennis ball	–	Tennisball
terrible	–	schrecklich
thanks	–	danke
thank you	–	danke
that	–	jener/jene/jenes
that's right	–	ganz recht/stimmt
theatre	–	Theater
there	–	da/dort
there are	–	dort sind/es gibt
there is	–	dort ist/es gibt
these	–	diese
thin	–	dünn
things	–	Dinge/Sachen
(to) think	–	denken
this	–	dieser/diese/dieses
those	–	jene
through	–	durch
(to) throw	–	werfen
ticket	–	Fahrkarte/Eintrittskarte
(to) tie	–	binden
time	–	Zeit
timetable	–	Fahrplan
title	–	Titel
to	–	zu/nach
today	–	heute
together	–	zusammen
tomb	–	Grab
tomorow	–	morgen
tonight	–	heute Abend
too	–	auch
top	–	Spitze/Gipfel
tortoise	–	Schildkröte
towards	–	auf ... zu
tower	–	Turm
town	–	Stadt
toy box	–	Spielzeugkiste
tractor	–	Traktor
traffic lights	–	Ampel
train	–	Zug
by train	–	mit dem Zug
train driver	–	Lokomotivführer
treasure room	–	Schatzkammer
tree	–	Baum
trousers	–	Hose
(to) try	–	versuchen
(to) turn (left/right)	–	(links/rechts) abbiegen
twins	–	Zwillinge
umbrella	–	Regenschirm
uncle	–	Onkel
under (the)	–	unter
Underground	–	U-Bahn
uniform	–	Uniform
until	–	bis
upstairs	–	oben
(to) use	–	benutzen/nutzen
usually	–	gewöhnlich
very	–	sehr
video	–	Video
village	–	Dorf
(to) visit	–	besuchen
volleyball	–	Volleyball
Wales	–	Wales
waltzer	–	Fahrt auf dem Volksfest
(to) wait	–	warten
(to) wake up	–	aufwachen
(a) walk	–	Spaziergang
(to) walk	–	(zu Fuß) gehen
Walkman	–	Walkman
wall	–	Wand
(to) want	–	wollen
warm	–	warm
(to) wash	–	waschen
(to) wash up	–	spülen
(to) watch	–	ansehen/zusehen
watch	–	Armbanduhr
water	–	Wasser
weather	–	Wetter
week	–	Woche
what	–	welcher/-e/-es/was
wheel	–	Rad
when	–	wann
where	–	wo
where from	–	woher
which	–	welcher/-e/-es
white	–	weiß
who	–	wer

195

Anhang: Schwierige Wörter, die wir in diesem Buch benutzen

whose	–	wessen
why	–	warum
window	–	Fenster
winner	–	Gewinner
with	–	mit/dabei
without	–	ohne
work	–	Arbeit
(to) work	–	arbeiten
woman	–	Frau
wonderful	–	wunderschön

(oh) wonderful!	–	toll
(to) write	–	schreiben
... years old	–	... Jahre alt
yellow	–	gelb
yesterday	–	gestern
(not) yet	–	noch nicht
zebra crossing	–	Zebrastreifen
zoo	–	Zoo

Anhang: Schwierige Wörter, die wir in diesem Buch benutzen

16.2 Deutsch – Englisch

Deutsch		Englisch
(links/rechts)		
abbiegen	–	(to) turn (left/right)
Abend	–	evening
aber	–	but
abfahren	–	(to) depart
abfliegen	–	(hier) (to) leave
Abflug	–	departure
abschließen	–	(to) lock
(die) Absicht		
haben zu	–	(to) be going to
Abtei	–	abbey
Adresse	–	address
Affe	–	monkey
alt	–	old
Amerika	–	America
Amerikaner(in)	–	American
amerikanisch	–	American
Ampel	–	traffic lights
(der, die, das)		
andere	–	(the) other
Anfang	–	start/beginning
angeln	–	(to) fish
anhalten	–	(to) stop
Anhaltspunkt	–	clue
ankommen	–	(to) arrive
Ankunft	–	arrival
anrufen	–	(to) phone
ansehen	–	(to) look at
Antwort	–	answer
Anweisung	–	instruction
Apfel	–	apple
Arbeit	–	work
arbeiten	–	(to) work
Arm	–	arm
Armbanduhr	–	watch
Arzt/Ärztin	–	doctor
Assistent(in)	–	assistant
Astronaut(in)	–	astronaut
auch	–	too
auf	–	on
auf (mit Akk.)	–	onto
auf ... zu	–	towards
auf der linken		
Seite	–	on the left
auf der rechten		
Seite	–	on the right
aufwachen	–	(to) wake up
Auge	–	eye
außerhalb	–	outside
aussteigen	–	(to) get off
Australien	–	Australia
Auto	–	car
Autobahn	–	motorway
Autoscooter	–	dodgem car
Baby	–	baby
Bäcker	–	baker
Bäckerei	–	bakery
Bahnhof	–	station
Bahnsteig	–	platform
Bahnübergang	–	level crossing
bald	–	soon
Ball	–	ball
Banane	–	banana
bank	–	bank
Baseball	–	baseball
Basketball-		
mannschaft	–	basketball team
Basketballspiel	–	basketball game (match)
Bau	–	building
bauen	–	(to) build
Bauernhof	–	farm
Baum	–	tree
(be)enden	–	(to) end
beginnen	–	(to) begin/(to) start
Bein	–	leg
bekommen	–	(to) get
belegtes Brot	–	sandwich
bellen	–	(to) bark
benötigen	–	(to) need
benutzen	–	(to) use
Benzin	–	petrol
Berg	–	mountain
berühmt	–	famous
besitzen	–	has/have got
Besitzer	–	owner
besuchen	–	(to) visit
Bett	–	bed
Bild	–	(a) painting/picture
billig	–	cheap
binden	–	(to) tie
bis	–	until
bitte	–	please
Blätter	–	leaves
blau	–	blue
Bleistift	–	pencil
Blume	–	flower
Boot	–	boat

197

Anhang: Schwierige Wörter, die wir in diesem Buch benutzen

brauchen	–	(to) need	einkaufen gehen	– (to) go) shopping
Brot	–	bread	Eisenbahn	– railway
Brief	–	letter	einschalten	– (to) switch on
Briefmarke	–	stamp	einsteigen	– (to) get in /(to) get onto
Briefträger	–	postman	Eintrittskarte	– ticket
Brille	–	(pair of) glasses	Eis	– ice-cream
bringen	–	(to) bring	Elefant	– elephant
Brücke	–	bridge	Eltern	– parents
Bruder	–	brother	(am) Ende	
Buch	–	book	von ...	– at the end of ...
Bücherei	–	library	Engländer(in)	– hier: English
Bücherregale	–	bookshelves	englisch	– English
Burg	–	castle	s. entscheiden	– (to) decide
Büro	–	office	Entschuldigung	– (to be) sorry
Bürste	–	brush	(die) Erde	– (the) Earth
Bus	–	bus	(einen Zug)	
Bushaltestelle	–	bus stop	erreichen	– (to) catch (a train)
Butterbrot	–	sandwich	erster /-e /-es	– first
			erzählen	– (to) tell
Café	–	café	es gibt	– there is /there are
Clown	–	clown	essen	– (to) eat
Comic(heft)	–	comic		
Computer	–	computer	fahren	– (to) drive (ride a
Cousin(e)	–	cousin		bike /motorbike)
			Fahrer	– driver
da	–	there	Fahrplan	– timetable
dabei	–	with	Fahrrad	– bicycle /bike
Dach	–	roof	Fahrkarte	– ticket
Dampfeisenbahn	–	steam train	Fahrt (auf dem	
danke	–	thanks /thank you	Volksfest)	– fair ride (ride)
denken	–	(to) think	Familie	– family
deutsch	–	German	fangen	– (to) catch
Deutsche(r)	–	German	Farbe	– colour
Deutschland	–	Germany	Fax	– fax
diese	–	these	Fenster	– window
diese /dieser /			Ferien	– holidays
dieses	–	this	Fernsehen	– television
dieselbe Stelle	–	the same place	finden	– (to) find
Dinge	–	things	Fisch	– fish
Dom	–	cathedral	Flasche	– bottle
dort	–	there	fliegen	– (to) fly
dort drüben	–	over there	Flughafen	– airport
dort hinüber	–	over there	Flugzeug	– plane
dort ist	–	there is	Fluss	– river
dort sind	–	there are	Foto	– photo(graph)
Drache	–	kite	Fotos machen	– (to) take photographs
dünn	–	thin	Frage	– (a) question
durch	–	through	fragen	– (to) ask
dürfen	–	may	Frankreich	– France
			französisch	– French
Ecke	–	corner	Frau	– woman
Ei	–	egg	Freund(in)	– friend
Einbrecher	–	burglar	Freund	– boyfriend
Einbruch	–	burglary	frisch	– fresh
Eingang	–	entrance	Frosch	– frog

Anhang: Schwierige Wörter, die wir in diesem Buch benutzen

früh	–	early
Frühstück	–	breakfast
Fuchs	–	fox
Füller	–	pen
für	–	for
Fuß (Füße)	–	foot (feet)
Fußball	–	football
Fußballmannschaft	–	football team
Fußballspiel	–	football match
Fußballspieler	–	footballer
Fußboden	–	floor
Futter	–	food
füttern	–	(to) feed
Garage	–	garage
Garten	–	garden
Gebäude	–	building
geben	–	(to) give
geboren	–	born
Geburtstag	–	birthday
gefallen	–	(to) like
gegenüber	–	opposite
gehen	–	(to) go
(zu Fuß) gehen	–	(to) walk
Geisterbahn	–	ghost train
gelb	–	yellow
Geld	–	money
gemacht aus	–	made of
Gemälde	–	painting
geradeaus	–	straight on
gestern	–	yesterday
Geschenk	–	present
Geschichte	–	story
Getränk	–	drink
gewöhnlich	–	usually
Gewinner	–	winner
Gipfel	–	top
Giraffe	–	giraffe
Glas	–	glass
Gleis	–	platform
glücklich	–	lucky / happy
Glück haben	–	to be lucky
Gold	–	gold
Golf	–	golf
Grab	–	tomb
Gras	–	grass
Grönland	–	Greenland
Großstadt	–	city
groß	–	tall / large / big
Großeltern	–	grandparents
Großmutter	–	grandmother
Großvater	–	grandfather
grün	–	green
gucken	–	(to) look
Gürtel	–	belt
gut	–	good
Haar / Haare	–	hair
haben	–	(to) have / have got
Hafen	–	harbour
Hals	–	neck
halten	–	(to) hold
Hand	–	hand
Handschuhe	–	gloves
Hauptmahlzeit	–	dinner
Hauptstraße	–	main road
Haus	–	house
(zu) Hause	–	(at) home
Hausaufgaben	–	homework
Haustier	–	pet
heißen	–	(to be) called
Heizkörper	–	radiator
helfen	–	(to) help
Hemd	–	shirt
um ... herum	–	round
herunterhelfen	–	(to) help down
heute	–	today
heute Abend	–	tonight
hinein	–	into
hinter	–	behind
Hirsch	–	deer
Hobby	–	hobby
hoch	–	high
Hocker	–	stool
hoffen	–	(to) hope
Höhle	–	cave
holen	–	(to) fetch
hören	–	(to) listen
Hose	–	trousers
Hotel	–	hotel
hübsch	–	pretty
Hubschrauber	–	helicopter
Hund	–	dog
hüpfen	–	(to) hop
Hut	–	hat
Idee	–	idea
Igel	–	hedgehog
immer	–	always
in	–	into / in
in der Mitte	–	in the middle
Indien	–	India
Ingenieur	–	engineer
innen	–	inside
Insel	–	island
interessant	–	interesting
Irland	–	Ireland
Jacke	–	jacket

199

Anhang: Schwierige Wörter, die wir in diesem Buch benutzen

Deutsch		Englisch
Jahre alt	–	years old
jeder/-e/-es	–	every
jene	–	those
jener/jene/jenes	–	that
jetzt	–	now
joggen	–	(to) jog
Junge	–	boy
kalt	–	cold
Kamel	–	camel
Kamera	–	camera
kämpfen	–	(to) fight
Känguru	–	kangaroo
Karte	–	map
Kartoffel	–	potato
Karton	–	box
Käse	–	cheese
Kassette	–	cassette
Kathedrale	–	cathedral
Katze	–	cat
kaufen	–	(to) buy
kein Problem	–	no problem
Keks	–	biscuit
Kilt	–	kilt
Kind (Kinder)	–	child (children)
Kino	–	cinema
Kirche	–	church
Kirmes	–	(a) fair
Klasse	–	class
Kleid	–	dress
Kleidung	–	clothes
klein	–	small
klettern	–	(to) climb
Klingel	–	bell
klingeln	–	(to) ring
klopfen an ...	–	(to) knock at
Koch/Köchin	–	cook
kochen	–	(to) cook
Koffer	–	suitcase
Kokosnuss	–	coconut
kommen	–	(to) come
kommen aus	–	(to) come from
König	–	king
Königin	–	queen
können	–	can
Konzert	–	concert
Kopf	–	head
Körper	–	body
kosten	–	(to) cost
krank	–	ill
Kreisverkehr	–	roundabout
Krokodil	–	crocodile
Kreis	–	circle
Küche	–	kitchen
Kreuzung	–	crossing/junction
Kuchen	–	cake
Kuh	–	cow
kühl	–	cool
Kühlschrank	–	fridge
sich kümmern um	–	(to) look after
Kurs	–	course
kurz	–	short
Laden	–	shop
Lampe	–	lamp
Land	–	country
lang	–	long
langweilig	–	boring
Lärm	–	noise
lass/lasst uns	–	let's
Latein	–	Latin
laufen	–	(to) run
laut	–	loud
Leben	–	life (lives)
Lebensmittel	–	food
legen	–	(to) put
Lehrer(in)	–	teacher
leicht	–	easy
leise	–	(to be) quiet
lernen	–	(to) learn
lesen	–	(to) read
Leuchtturm	–	lighthouse
Leute	–	people
Licht	–	light
Liebe/r ...	–	Dear ...
Lieblings...	–	favourite
Lied	–	song
liegen	–	(to) lie
Limonade	–	lemonade
links	–	left
Loch	–	hole
Lokomotivführer	–	train driver
machen	–	(to) make/(to) do
Mädchen	–	girl
malen	–	(to) paint
manchmal	–	sometimes
Mann	–	man
Mantel	–	coat
Markt	–	market
Marktplatz	–	market place
Maus	–	mouse
Meer	–	sea
mehr	–	more
Menschen	–	people
Meter	–	metre
Milch	–	milk
Minute	–	minute
mit	–	with

Anhang: Schwierige Wörter, die wir in diesem Buch benutzen

jdn. mitnehmen	–	(to) take (someone)	Packung	–	packet
(in der) Mitte	–	in the middle	Park	–	park
Mittagessen	–	lunch	parken	–	(to) park
Mittagszeit	–	lunchtime	Parkplatz	–	car park
mögen	–	(to) like	Party	–	party
Monat	–	month	Pferd	–	horse
Monster	–	monster	Pflanze	–	plant
Morgen	–	morning	phantastisch	–	fantastic
Motorrad	–	motorbike	Pier	–	pier
Mund	–	mouth	Pilot	–	pilot
Musik	–	music	Plan	–	plan
Musiker	–	musician	planen	–	(to) plan
müssen	–	must	platter Reifen	–	flat tyre
Museum	–	museum	Polizeiauto	–	police car
Mutter	–	mother	Polizist(in)	–	policeman/policewoman
Mütze	–	hat	Pommes frites	–	chips
			Popgruppe	–	pop group
nach	–	after/to	Popkonzert	–	pop concert
Nacht	–	night	Post(amt)	–	post office
nächster/-e/-es	–	next	Postkarte	–	postcard
Nachmittag	–	afternoon	Prinz	–	prince
Nachbar	–	neighbour	Prinzessin	–	princess
nächstes Mal	–	next time	putzen	–	(to) clean
nahe	–	near	Pyramide	–	pyramid
(in der) Nähe (von)	–	near	Rad	–	wheel
Name	–	name	Radio	–	radio
Nase	–	nose	Rad fahren	–	(to) cycle
natürlich	–	of course	Rakete	–	rocket
neben	–	next to	Rasen	–	grass
nebenan	–	next door to	Räuber	–	robber
nehmen	–	(to) take	rechts	–	right
nett	–	nice	reiten	–	(to) ride
neu	–	new	Reiter	–	horserider
nicht	–	not	Regal	–	shelf (pl. shelves)
nie	–	never	Regenschirm	–	umbrella
noch einer	–	another	Regen	–	rain
nochmals	–	again	rennen	–	(to) run
Nummer	–	number	reich	–	rich
nur	–	only	reparieren	–	(to) repair/(to) mend
nutzen	–	(to) use	Restaurant	–	restaurant
			rot	–	red
oben	–	upstairs	ruhig (sein)	–	(to be) quiet
oben auf	–	on top of	rund	–	round
oder	–	or			
offen	–	open	Sachen	–	things
öffnen	–	(to) open	sammeln	–	(to) collect
oft	–	often	Sandalen	–	sandals
ohne	–	without	Sänger(in)	–	singer
Ohr	–	ear	sauber machen	–	(to) clean
Oma	–	grandma	Sauna	–	sauna
Onkel	–	uncle	Schachtel	–	packet
Opa	–	grandad	Schaf	–	sheep
Orange	–	orange	Schal	–	scarf
Ort	–	place	Schatzkammer	–	treasure room

Anhang: Schwierige Wörter, die wir in diesem Buch benutzen

schicken	–	(to) send
schieben	–	(to) push
Schildkröte	–	tortoise
schlafen	–	(to) sleep
Schlafzimmer	–	bedroom
Schlange	–	snake
schließen	–	(to) shut/(to) close
Schlüssel	–	key
Schnecke	–	snail
Schnee	–	snow
schneien	–	(to) snow
schneiden	–	(to) cut
schnell	–	fast
Schokolade	–	chocolate
schön	–	beautiful
die Schotten	–	the Scottish
Schottland	–	Scotland
Schrank	–	cupboard
schrecklich	–	terrible
schreiben	–	(to) write
Schreibtisch	–	desk
Schuh	–	shoe
Schule	–	school
Schulkinder	–	schoolchildren
schwarz	–	black
Schwein	–	pig
schwer	–	difficult
Schwester	–	sister
schwierig	–	difficult
Schwimmbad	–	swimming pool
Schwimmen	–	swimming
schwimmen	–	(to) swim
Schwimm- unterricht	–	swimming course
schwindeln	–	(to) cheat
(der) See	–	lake
Seelöwe	–	sea lion
Seevogel	–	sea bird
segeln	–	(to) sail
sehen	–	(to) look/(to) see
sehr	–	very
Seite	–	side
Sekretär(in)	–	secretary
setzen	–	(to) put
Shorts	–	shorts
Silvester	–	New Year's Eve
singen	–	(to) sing
sitzen	–	(to) sit
Skateboard fahren	–	(to go) skateboarding
Ski laufen	–	(to) ski
so	–	so
Socken	–	socks
Sommer	–	summer
Sonne	–	sun
Sonnenbrille	–	sunglasses
Sonnenschein	–	sunshine
sorgen für	–	(to) look after
spannend	–	exciting
Spaß	–	fun
(zu) spät kommen	–	(to be) late
Spaziergang	–	(a) walk
Spiegel	–	mirror
Spiele	–	games
spielen	–	(to) play
Spielzeugkiste	–	toy box
Spinne	–	spider
Spitze	–	top
Sportzentrum	–	sports centre
sprechen	–	(to) speak
springen	–	(to) jump
spülen	–	(to) wash up
Squash	–	squash
Stadt	–	town
stecken	–	(to) put
stehen	–	(to) be /(to) stand
Stein	–	stone
Stelle	–	place
stellen	–	(to) put
Stockwerk	–	floor
Straße	–	street/road
Streifen	–	stripe
stimmt (ganz recht)	–	that's right
Stuhl	–	chair
südlich	–	south
Supermarkt	–	supermarket
Tag	–	day
Tante	–	aunt/aunty
Tänzer(in)	–	dancer
tanzen	–	(to) dance
Tasse	–	cup
Tasche	–	bag/pocket
Taxi	–	taxi
Tee	–	tea
Telefon	–	telephone
Telefonzelle	–	telephone box
Tennis	–	tennis
Tennisball	–	tennis ball
teuer	–	expensive
Theater	–	theatre
Tier	–	animal
Tisch	–	table
Titel	–	title
Tochter	–	daughter
toll	–	(hier) wonderful!
Tor	–	gate
Traktor	–	tractor

Anhang: Schwierige Wörter, die wir in diesem Buch benutzen

tragen	–	(to) carry	Walkman	– Walkman
treffen	–	(to) meet	Wand	– wall
treten	–	(to) kick	wann	– when
trinken	–	(to) drink	warm	– warm
trocknen	–	(to) dry	warten	– (to) wait
Tür	–	door	warum	– why
Turm	–	tower	was	– what
			waschen	– (to) wash
U-Bahn	–	the Underground	Wasser	– water
über	–	over/across	Weihnachten	– Christmas
überqueren	–	(to) cross	weil	– because
Uhr	–	clock	weinen	– (to) cry
umziehen	–	(to) move	weiß	– white
und	–	and	weit	– a long way
Unfall	–	accident	weiterer	– another
Uniform	–	uniform	welcher/-e/-es	– which/that
unter	–	under	wem	– who
unterhalten	–	(to) chat	wer	– who
Urlaub	–	holiday	werden	– (to) be going to
			werfen	– (to) throw
Vater	–	father	wessen	– whose
Vati	–	dad	Wetter	– weather
verändern	–	(to) change	wie	– how
verkaufen	–	(to) sell	wie viel	– how much
Verkäufer(in)	–	shop assistant	wie viele	– how many
vergessen	–	(to) forget	wissen	– (to) know
verlassen	–	(to) leave	wo	– where
verlieren	–	(to) lose	Woche	– week
versuchen	–	(to) try	woher	– where from
Video	–	video	wohnen	– (to) live/(to) stay
viel/viele	–	a lot of/lots of	wollen	– (to) want
viele	–	many	wunderschön	– wonderful
vielleicht	–	perhaps		
Vogel	–	bird	Zebrastreifen	– Zebra crossing
Volksfest	–	fair	zeichnen	– (to) draw
Volleyball	–	volleyball	Zeit	– time
von	–	from/by/of	Zeitung	– newspaper
vor	–	before	Zimmer	– room
Vormittag	–	morning	Zirkus	– circus
vorübergehend			Zoo	– zoo
wohnen	–	(to) stay	zu	– to
			Zug	– train
wach	–	awake	zusammen	– together
Wachen	–	guards	zusehen	– (to) watch
Wald	–	forest	Zwillinge	– twins
Wales	–	Wales		

Lösungen zu den Übungsaufgaben

In den Lösungen werden Lang- und Kurzformen der Verben verwendet. Natürlich sind jeweils beide Formen möglich. Wenn bei einer Übung ein Lösungssatz vorgegeben ist, richten sich die übrigen Lösungen nach dem Muster, z. B. Seite 16 Übung 1 a, *It's*... (Kurzform) oder Seite 25 Übung 3 a, *I am*... (Langform). Bei den meisten Übungen, bei denen kein Beispiel angegeben ist, ist die Kurzform gewählt worden.

Wo mehrere Antworten möglich sind, steht die beste Antwort ohne Klammern, weitere mögliche Antworten in Klammern.

Beispiel: This is Peter's coat. (his)
= This is his coat. (andere Möglichkeit)

Plural

1. a) book / books
   b) key / keys
   c) baby / babies
   d) suitcase / suitcases
   e) scarf / scarves
   f) city / cities
   g) camera / cameras
   h) sandwich / sandwiches
   i) glass / glasses
   j) child / children

2. (beliebige Reihenfolge)
   a) pens
   b) dresses
   c) bags
   d) brushes
   e) clocks
   f) glasses
   g) keys
   h) books
   i) umbrellas
   j) dogs

Lösungen zu den Übungsaufgaben

3.

[S]	[Z]	[IZ]
books	dogs	brushes
clocks	umbrellas	glasses
	keys	dresses
	bags	
	pens	

4. a) a tin of soup / two tins of soup
   b) a packet of biscuits / three packets of biscuits
   c) a box of pencils / four boxes of pencils
   d) a bar of chocolate / five bars of chocolate
   e) a bottle of lemonade / six bottles of lemonade
   f) a pair of sunglasses / seven pairs of sunglasses

5. a) George has got four buckets of milk.
   b) Barbara has got two boxes of puzzles.
   c) Anne has got a packet of bird food.
   d) Tom has got three bottles of water.
   e) Grandfather has got a bar of chocolate.
   f) Grandmother has got six (eight) pairs of jeans (trousers).

6. a) Mary eats a packet of biscuits.
   b) John buys two bottles of milk.
   c) Mrs Sampson washes sixteen pairs of trousers!

Groß- und Kleinschreibung

1. Please read this fax. It is from Elizabeth and me in America. We're waiting for a plane to London with Tom Mcdonald from Scotland. Tom has got photos of Lucy and I have got the video of New York. See you tomorrow (Wednesday). Annabella

Lösungen zu den Übungsaufgaben

2. a) The fax is from Elizabeth and Annabella.
    b) Annabella writes the fax.
    c) They are in America.
    d) They are waiting for a plane to London.
    e) They (Elizabeth and Annabella) are with Tom Mcdonald.
    f) He (Tom Mcdonald) is from Scotland.
    g) No, she hasn't. Tom has got the photographs.
    h) The 'i' in the fax is Annabella.
    i) Annabella has got the video of New York.
    j) It is Tuesday.

3. (Du kannst diese Sätze auch in einer anderen Reihenfolge schreiben.)
    a) Mr Fox lives in West Road.
    b) Mrs Green lives in George Street.
    c) Miss Dixon lives in Bridge Avenue.
    d) Dr Graham lives in James Street.
    e) Joanne lives in Market Street.
    f) The cathedral is in The Market Square.
    g) The cinema is in Osborne Road.
    h) The market is in Back Street.
    i) The post office is in Low Road.
    j) The train station is in Bridge Street.
    k) Springwood High School is in Queensway.
    l) Mr Fox goes to the cinema on Saturdays.
    m) Mrs Green goes to the post office on Mondays.
    n) Miss Dixon goes to Springwood High School on Fridays.
    o) Dr Graham goes to the cathedral on Wednesdays.
    p) Joanne goes to the train station on Sundays.

4. a) The first book is The Clowns by Barry Fue. (March)
    b) The second book is Sea Birds by Lucy March. (April)
    c) The third book is Uniforms by P. Rail. (May)

Lösungen zu den Übungsaufgaben

d) The fourth book is Mrs Smith by June Worth. (July)
e) The fifth book is China by Ly Ju. (August)
f) The sixth book is Planes and Trains by A. U. Tugs. (September)
g) The seventh book is Cars by Seb. Temper. (October)
h) The eighth book is The Cat's Eye by Mike November. (December)

Genetiv

1. a) It's John's horse.
   b) It's Peter's plane.
   c) It's Carol's car.
   d) It's Arthur's coat.
   e) They're Amanda's dogs.
   f) They're Jackie's shoes.
   g) They're Kathy's glasses.

2. a) sisters'
   b) policemen's
   c) children's
   d) girls'
   e) footballers'
   f) parents'
   g) women's
   h) men's
   i) boys'

3. a) brothers'
   b) grandfather's
   c) Jackie's
   d) Robert's
   e) policeman's / Policewomen's
   f) grandmother's
   g) girls'
   h) women's
   i) Margaret's / teacher's / boy's (boys') / girl's (girls') / schoolchildren's
   j) cat's

4. a) the corner of the table
   b) the window of the house
   c) the wheel of the motorbike
   d) the title of the book
   e) the door of the car
   f) the top of the mountain (hill)
   g) the seats of the bus

Lösungen zu den Übungsaufgaben

5. a) the foot of the bed
    c) the mouth of the river
    b) the leg of the table
    d) the arms of the chair

6. a) girl's bag
    c) cat's milk
    e) children's teacher
    g) man's hand
    i) women's basketball team
    k) boy's (boys') mother
    b) door of the shop
    d) map of Scotland
    f) pop group's new CD
    h) middle of the road
    j) Jack's book
    l) colour of the door

7. a) Carol's dog is big.
    b) The door of the house is red.
    c) The children's school is in Newcastle-upon-Tyne.
    d) The brothers' sister is called Mary.

Artikel

1. a) an
    c) a
    e) a
    g) a
    i) a
    b) a
    d) an
    f) a
    h) an
    j) an

2. (beliebige Reihenfolge)
a window / an eye / a banana / an apple / an ice-cream / an ear / a chair / a telephone / a door / an umbrella

3. a) I am a shop assistant.
    c) She is a pilot.
    e) She is a taxi driver.
    b) He is a policeman.
    d) He is a teacher.
    f) I am a singer.

4. a) She is a teacher.
    c) A house, an umbrella and a door.
    b) It is an apple.

Lösungen zu den Übungsaufgaben

5. a) the house   b) the elephant
    c) the book   d) the orange
    e) the girl   f) the USA
    g) the boy   h) the island
    i) the bus   j) the uniform

6. the house   the elephant
    the book   the orange
    the girl   the boy
    the island   the bus
    the USA   the uniform

Pronomen und Begleiter

1. a) He rides a horse.   b) It's very large.
    c) They're brother and sister. d) We're cousins.
    e) It's from Aberdeen.   f) She's an old cat.
    g) They go to school together. h) They wake Karen up in the morning.
    i) She plays golf.   j) We're good friends.
    k) It's small.   l) He's a taxi driver.
    m) They live in Wales.   n) She reads comics.

2. (Textreihenfolge)
    you / I / he / he / she / she / she / he / she / They / You / He / it / she

3. a) Wendy   b) Callum
    c) Nibbles   d) Arthur
    e) he   f) they
    g) she   h) it
    i) we
    (Wolkenkratzer) a = Wendy / f = they / i = we / b = Callum / d = Arthur / g = she / h = it / c = Nibbles / e = he

Lösungen zu den Übungsaufgaben

4. Newcastle

   Beispiele:

5. a) We can visit him today.
   b) Give her the newspaper, please.
   c) Can you take us to the pop concert?
   d) I have a good name for it.
   e) Carol buys him a new coat.
   f) I can see them tomorrow.
   g) "I want you to watch Robin Hood."

6. (Textreihenfolge) me / him / them / them / him / them / him / them / you

7. a) me   b) us
   c) you   d) her / them
   e) them   f) you
   g) him   h) me

Lösungen zu den Übungsaufgaben

    i) you   j) him
    k) you

8.
- a) Zoe has (has got) a letter for you.
- b) Ruth takes (drives) us to school.
- c) Can you phone me, please?
- d) Perhaps they can visit us.
- e) He meets her today. (He's meeting her today.)
- f) Peter has got a new car. He is washing it.
- g) She goes to the cinema with him.
- h) Sharon's dog is little (small), can you see it?

9.
- a) First, she talks to her.
- b) She asks her to help.
- c) She talks to him.
- d) He can't drive them to the airport.
- e) He asks him to help.
- f) He can help them.
- g) They meet him at 4.00 p.m.
- h) They go to the airport with him.
- i) She thanks him.

10.
- a) My
- b) my
- c) Her
- d) His
- e) My
- f) Our
- g) my / Her
- h) My / our
- i) Their

11.
- a) our / My / her
- b) their
- c) your
- d) -----
- e) my / its
- f) my
- g) My / her (his)

12.
- a) Our big dog.
- b) Their new lives in America.
- c) My garden.
- d) Her (Their) brother and his friends.

Lösungen zu den Übungsaufgaben

13. a) His / its b) Her / she
    c) Their / They d) We / us / We / them
    e) our / we / they f) His / He
    g) My / it h) I

h comes from AMERICA

14. a) This is a cat. That is a dog.
    b) This is a pencil. That is a pen.
    c) This is a policeman. That is a doctor.
    d) This is a door. That is a window.
    e) This is an apple. That is a banana.
    f) This is a book. That is a letter.
    g) This is a tree. That is a forest.

15. (Die Subjekte eines Satzes sind austauschbar.)
    a) This is Tricia and that is Robin.
    b) This is a French book and that is a Latin book.
    c) This is a cup and that is a glass.
    d) This is my dad (father / brother) and that is my mum (mother / sister).
    e) This is an English car and that is a German car.
    f) This is George and that is Amanda.
    g) This is a red pen and that is a green pen.

16. a) These are tennis balls. Those are footballs.
    b) These are cars. Those are bicycles (bikes).

Lösungen zu den Übungsaufgaben

c) These are feet. Those are hands.
d) These are pens. Those are pencils.
e) These are gloves. Those are shoes.
f) These are bananas. Those are apples.

17. a) These are blue jeans and those are black trousers.
b) These are long coats and those are short jackets.
c) These are shirts and those are T-shirts.
d) These are cheap socks and those are expensive socks.
e) These are Bermuda shorts and those are football shorts.
f) These are summer (cool) shoes and those are sandals.

18. a) This is / those are   b) These are / That is
    c) This is / that is   d) These are / those are
    e) This is / those are   f) This is / that is

Ortsangaben

1. a) The girl is in front of Braybrook Hall.
   b) The big car is in front of Braybrook Hall.
   c) The flowers are behind Braybrook Hall.
   d) The table is behind Braybrook Hall.
   e) The trousers are behind Braybrook Hall.
   f) The bicycle is in front of Braybrook Hall.
   g) The tree is in front of Braybrook Hall.
   h) The police car is behind Braybrook Hall.
   i) The horse is in front of Braybrook Hall.

2. a) The elephant is behind the giraffe.
   b) The car is in front of the supermarket.

Lösungen zu den Übungsaufgaben

3. a) Patricia is sitting next to the telephone.
   b) Tom is standing near the railway.
   c) Carol lives next door to John.
   d) Tina and Charles are reading next to the radio.
   e) Grandma is sleeping near (next to) the television.
   f) The bakery is next door to the post office.

4. a) The ball is next to the tree.
   b) The dog is near the girl.
   c) The policeman lives next door to the teacher.

5. a) The bus is outside the toy box.
   b) The car is outside the toy box.
   c) The elephant is inside the toy box.
   d) The telephone is inside the toy box.
   e) The plane is outside the toy box.
   f) The shop is inside the toy box.
   g) The house is outside the toy box.
   h) The ball is outside the toy box.
   i) The clown is inside the toy box.
   j) The train is inside the toy box.

6. a) The bottles are outside the houses.
   b) The television is inside the shop.
   c) Robert's sandwiches are in his bag.

Lösungen zu den Übungsaufgaben

7. a) The chocolate is under the desk.
   b) The lemonade is on top of the desk.
   c) The tennis ball is under the desk.
   d) Jenny's present is under the desk.
   e) The newspaper is under the desk.
   f) The camera is on top of the desk.
   g) The hat is on top of the desk.
   h) The French book is on top of the desk.
   i) The pencils are under the desk.

8. a) My car is on the left.
   b) Mike is on the right.
   c) June is in the middle of the river.
   d) The spider is on the left.
   e) The flower is in the middle.
   f) The telephone box is on the left.

9. a) John's photo is in the middle.
   b) The telephone is on the left.
   c) James is on the right.

10.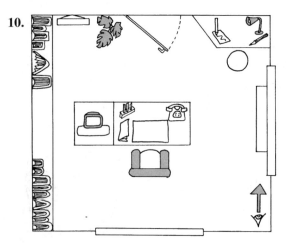

Lösungen zu den Übungsaufgaben

11. a) The door is next to the plant (the drawing table).
b) Your (The) computer is on top of the computer table.
c) Your (The) drawing table is next to the door.
d) Your (The) stool is behind the drawing table.
e) The lamp is on top of the drawing table.

12. a) at b) at
c) across d) across
e) at f) Across
g) At h) at
i) across j) at

13. a) The post office is across the road (street).
b) Paula meets Ian at the station (railway / train station).
c) Carol mustn't go (walk) across the grass.

14. a) Amanda is in the café.
b) The car is in the garage.
c) Peter is going into the shop.
d) Mr and Mrs Little are getting into their car.
e) John's keys are in his pocket.
f) Grandad is putting a cassette into his Walkman.
g) Mr Smith is going into the post office.
h) Julia's camera is in her (the) car.
i) A robber is in the bank.
j) More robbers are going into the bank.

15. a) on b) on
c) onto d) onto
e) on f) onto
g) onto h) on
i) on (onto) j) onto (on)

Lösungen zu den Übungsaufgaben

16. a) Allan is getting onto a bus.

b) Mrs Pringle always leaves her keys on the table.

c) Oliver walks (goes) on a bridge.

d) They're running onto the road.

17. a) goes to the market

b) driving towards the park.

c) flying to America.

d) walking towards the house.

e) going to Durham.

f) reading the timetable of the train to Glasgow.

18. a) Can you go to the supermarket?

b) Carol is driving towards the station.

c) Valerie and Jeremy are walking to Keswick.

d) On Mondays Peter goes to the cinema.

19. a) (Textreihenfolge) across / to / next to / in front of / towards
Quadrat = 2 e

b) (Textreihenfolge) into / Inside / under / in the middle / near / Behind
Quadrat = 2 c

c) (Textreihenfolge) outside / next to / on the left / towards / on top of / to
Quadrat = 5 b

d) (Textreihenfolge) into / across / On / behind / into

20. (Musterlösung)

a) First go straight on, then turn left down Long Road and the post office is on the left.

b) First go straight on, then turn left down Long Road and the school is on the right (next to the shop).

c) First go straight on, then turn right down Green Lane and the cinema is on the left.

d) First go straight on, then turn right down Park Lane, after that turn left into Park Avenue and the bus station is on the left.

Lösungen zu den Übungsaufgaben

e) First go straight on, then turn right down Green Lane and the park is on the right.

f) First go straight on, then turn left down Station Road and the Centre Hotel is on the left.

21. (Musterlösung)

a) First turn left into Abbott Street, then go straight on until North Road. Turn left down North Road and then take the first street right, Long Road, and the museum is on the right.

b) First go straight on, then turn right down Gate Street and the cathedral is on the right.

c) First go straight on until Sea View, then turn left and the theatre is on the right.

d) First go straight on until Low Road, then turn right down Low Road. After that, turn first left down Castle Street and the castle is on your left.

e) First go straight on, then turn left down Harbour Road and the old harbour is on the right.

f) First go straight on, then turn left down Bridge Street. Go across the river and then turn left into Cliff Road. After that go straight on and then take the first left onto the pier. The lighthouse is at the end of the pier.

g) First go straight on, then turn right down Cliff Road. Next, turn left into Old Avenue and the church is on the left.

h) First go straight on, then turn left. Next, turn left and then right down River Road and the river is on the right.

i) First go straight on, then turn left into Bridge Street. After that, go across the river and then take the second road on the left. Go down Kipper Lane and the railway museum is on the right.

j) First go straight on, then turn left into Railway Road. After that, take the first turning right into Abbott Street and then the first left into the bus station.

22. a) Red Lane   b) Low Road
    c) Kipper Lane   d) Little Market Place

Lösungen zu den Übungsaufgaben

23. (Musterlösung)
a) Go straight on to the end. Turn right. Turn left. Take the second left. Take the first right. You're there.
b) Go straight on to the end. Turn right. Go straight on again to the end. You're there.
c) Go straight on. Turn right. Turn right again. Turn left. Turn right. Go straight on. You're there.
d) Go straight on. Turn right. Turn right again. Take the second right. Turn left. Turn left again. Go straight on. You're there.
e) Go straight on. Turn left. Go straight on. Turn left again. Take the third right. Turn left. Go straight on. You're there.

24.
a) motorway
b) level crossing
c) traffic lights
d) roundabout
e) junction
f) zebra crossing
g) bridge

Zahlen, Datums- und Zeitangaben

1.
a) six + twenty-five = thirty-one
b) one hundred and one + eighty-four = one hundred and eighty-five
c) three hundred and eleven + ninety-seven = four hundred and eight
d) one hundred and twenty-nine – seventeen = one hundred and twelve
e) seven hundred and sixty-seven – twenty = seven hundred and forty-seven
f) six hundred and fifty-seven – three hundred and forty-three = three hundred and fourteen

2.

¹1	2	²3	■	³7	7
0	■	⁴6	3	1	■
⁵3	⁶8	1	■	⁷1	⁸5
■	5	■	⁹4	■	6
¹⁰2	■	¹¹2	■	¹²6	■
¹³1	¹⁴4	■	¹⁵2	0	¹⁶5
■	¹⁷8	9	1	■	1
¹⁸1	2	■	¹⁹6	7	8

3.
a) seven hundred and twenty
b) one hundred and sixteen
c) three hundred and eighty-four
d) twenty-six
e) four hundred and one

4.
1st spider   6th fox
2nd tortoise   7th deer
3rd hedgehog   8th mouse
4th snake   9th frog
5th snail   10th cat

The snail is fifth.
The mouse is eighth.
The snake is fourth.
The tortoise is second.
The deer is seventh.
The cat is tenth.
The spider is first.
The frog is ninth.
The hedgehog is third.
The fox is sixth.

Lösungen zu den Übungsaufgaben

5. The Eiffel Tower

6. (Andere Möglichkeiten stehen in Klammern.)
The first letter is the fifth (33rd) on the left.
The second letter is the tenth on the left. (16th / 17th or 27th on the right)
The third letter is the twenty-eighth (40th) on the right.
The fourth letter is the sixteenth (17th / 27th) on the right (2nd on the left).
The sixth letter is the fortieth (28th) on the right.

7.
a) seventeen minutes past five   b) five to nine
c) half past three   d) six o'clock
e) twenty-five to three   f) twenty-three minutes to ten
g) (a) quarter to five   h) twenty past eleven

8.
a) wake up   6.00 a.m.
b) eat breakfast   7.00 a.m.
c) have a drink   9.45 a.m.
d) have lunch   12.30 p.m.
e) start work after lunch 1.20 p.m.
f) go home   6.00 p.m.
g) watch television   7.00 p.m.
h) go to sleep   10.30 p.m.

9. departures

BA 3458	Frankfurt	7.11
KLM 456	Amsterdam	9.15
LH 736	New York	9.51
ZU 297	Zurich	10.45
WI 727	Trinidad	16.09

arrivals

JT 784	Cairo	6.20
TWA 114	Chicago	10.30
PA 335	Madrid	17.32
ST 926	Paris	19.19
SK 555	Oslo	23.57

Lösungen zu den Übungsaufgaben

10. a) The plane from Cairo arrives at six twenty.
    b) The plane to Frankfurt leaves at seven eleven.
    c) The plane to Amsterdam leaves at nine fifteen.
    d) The plane to New York leaves at nine fifty-one.
    e) The plane from Chicago arrives at ten thirty.
    f) The plane to Zurich leaves at ten forty-five.
    g) The plane to Trinidad leaves at sixteen oh-nine.
    h) The plane from Madrid arrives at seventeen thirty-two.
    i) The plane from Paris arrives at nineteen nineteen.
    j) The plane from Oslo arrives at twenty-three fifty-seven.

11. a) March   b) February
    c) September   d) December
    e) August   f) April

12. a) Jenny's birthday is on 21st January.
    b) Grandad's birthday is on 13th March.
    c) Our holiday in Paris is on 17th May.
    d) My swimming course is on 31st October.
    e) My school visit to London is on 2nd November.
    f) The Christmas concert at the theatre is on 15th December.

13. a) Halloween is on 31st October.
    b) Guy Fawkes Night is on 5th November.
    c) New Year's Eve is on 31st December.
    d) Boxing Day is on 26th December.

14. a) Simone's grandfather: in nineteen fifteen.
    b) Simone's grandmother: in nineteen twenty.
    c) Simone's father: in nineteen forty-five.
    d) Simone's mother: in nineteen forty-seven.
    e) Simone's brother: in nineteen sixty-nine.

Lösungen zu den Übungsaufgaben

f) Simone's sister: in nineteen seventy-four.

g) Simone's daughter: in nineteen ninety-four.

15. (beliebige Reihenfolge)

    a) Thursday   b) Tuesday
    c) Friday   d) Sunday
    e) Wednesday

16. a) Monday   b) Saturday

17. Sunday   They go to the circus.
    Monday   They go to Holts farm.
    Tuesday   They go on a helicopter.
    Wednesday   They go to Larks Park.
    Thursday   They go to the castle.
    Friday   They go to the swimming pool.
    Saturday   They go on (to) the steam train.

Adverbien der Zeit und Häufigkeit

1. a) Peter usually rides his bicycle.
    b) She often plays tennis.
    c) We can sometimes visit grandma in America.
    d) Mary always watches television.
    e) Lucy and Susan usually sit together.
    f) Tony never drives to work.
    g) You must never run across the road.
    h) John sometimes goes swimming.
    i) They often fly to Australia.

2. a) Henry often goes to the cinema.
    b) Henry always watches television.
    c) Henry sometimes visits a restaurant.

Lösungen zu den Übungsaufgaben

d) Henry never goes swimming.
e) Henry always works with a computer.
f) Nina never goes to the cinema.
g) Nina usually watches television.
h) Nina never visits a restaurant.
i) Nina often goes swimming.
j) Nina sometimes works with a computer.
k) Lucinda sometimes goes to the cinema.
l) Lucinda often watches television.
m) Lucinda often visits a restaurant.
n) Lucinda usually goes swimming.
o) Lucinda never works with a computer.
p) Barry usually goes to the cinema.
q) Barry never watches television.
r) Barry sometimes visits a restaurant.
s) Barry often goes swimming.
t) Barry sometimes works with a computer.

3. a) On Mondays Paula goes to the library.
   Paula goes to the library on Mondays.
   b) On Tuesdays Jim and Zoe eat at the Luxus restaurant.
   Jim and Zoe eat at the Luxus restaurant on Tuesdays.
   c) Every night Jane reads a book.
   Jane reads a book every night.
   d) On Saturdays Trevor washes his car.
   Trevor washes his car on Saturdays.
   e) Every day Kim plays golf.
   Kim plays golf every day.
   f) Every evening Carol and Mike ride their bicycles.
   Carol and Mike ride their bicycles every evening.
   g) On Sundays Peter makes breakfast.
   Peter makes breakfast on Sundays.

h) On Fridays Andy buys a newspaper.
   Andy buys a newspaper on Fridays.
i) Every morning Paul drives to work.
   Paul drives to work every morning.
j) On Wednesdays I do my homework.
   I do my homework on Wednesdays.

4. a) (On Mondays) Carol goes to the supermarket in Cambridge on Mondays.
   b) We often visit Lucy in London.
   c) Every morning James has (eats) cornflakes for breakfast.
   d) Every afternoon Mr and Mrs Archer walk (go) to the park.
   e) She usually drinks water.

5. a) I always run home from school.
   b) On Mondays Laura and I play tennis in Cheltenham.
   c) Every day I listen to my radio.
   d) Every morning I go swimming before breakfast.
   e) I go shopping with my father on Tuesdays.
   f) My sister visits our grandparents on Thursdays.
   g) My parents often take my dog for a walk.
   h) Every afternoon I ride Amanda's horse.
   i) Aunty Caroline sometimes takes June to a football match.
   j) I never watch television.
   k) On Fridays I eat my lunch in a café.
   l) I can usually use my sister's bicycle.

Zeitformen des Verbs

1. a) plays
   b) likes
   c) fly
   d) climb
   e) eats
   f) carries
   g) ride
   h) repair
   i) goes
   j) watches
   k) look
   l) writes

2. a) Fiona plays squash.
   b) I write letters.
   c) Grandad sits in the garden.

3. a) usually makes
   b) never buys
   c) jog every day
   d) goes / on Saturdays
   e) always sleeps
   f) sometimes catches
   g) often walk to school

4. a) Every day we swim in the sea.
   b) I sometimes read a newspaper (Sometimes I read a newspaper.)
   c) We never cook. We always eat in a restaurant.

5. a) swim / have / drive
   b) reads / watches
   c) play / eat
   d) goes / waits / walk
   e) has / read / goes
   f) find / open / close / switch on / are

6. First look right, then left and then right again, and then go (walk) across the road.

Lösungen zu den Übungsaufgaben

7. a) Mrs Graham is not a teacher. (isn't)
    b) Julie is not old. (isn't)
    c) Martin and Mary are not tall. (aren't)
    d) Mr and Mrs King are not American. (aren't)
    e) I am not a doctor. (I'm not)
    f) The bus is not white. (isn't)
    g) We are not cooks. (aren't / We're not)

8. a) The cat isn't black. (is not)   b) I'm not John. (am not)
    c) They aren't new CDs. (are not / They're not)

9. a) He doesn't want a bike.   b) It doesn't stop at Durham.
    c) He doesn't live here.   d) They don't watch television.
    e) We don't go to London.   f) She doesn't drive a new car.
    g) She doesn't drink lemonade.   h) I don't like cats.

10. a) I don't like apples.   b) We don't eat bananas.
    c) He doesn't drink milk.

11. a) Morton manor isn't 70 meters high.
    b) This door isn't made of gold.
    c) We don't sell books in the Manor.
    d) Mr and Mrs Pedigree don't live in the Manor.
    e) The paintings aren't new.
    f) The Manor isn't 500 years old and I'm not 50 years old on Monday.
    g) On Wednesdays Michael doesn't clean the windows.
    h) The ghost isn't a woman.
    i) Samantha doesn't look after the horses.

12. a) Do / buy   b) Does / go
    c) Does / go   d) Do / use
    e) Do / stop   f) Do / sit
    g) Does / wear   h) Does / have

Lösungen zu den Übungsaufgaben

13. a) Do / you / Yes, I do.   b) Does / rain / No, it doesn't.
c) Do / need / Yes, you do.   d) Do / visit / No, we don't.
e) Does / stop / No, it doesn't.   f) Do / go / Yes, you (we) do.
g) Does / live / Yes, she does.   h) Do / drink / No, they don't.

14. lie – lying
eat – eating
wash – washing
drive – driving
hope – hoping
sit – sitting
visit – visiting
catch – catching

15. a) sleeping.   b) is fishing.
c) is singing.   d) The / are flying.
e) The / is writing a letter.   f) The cook is sailing.
g) are playing.

16. a) Today it's raining.   b) Debbie is sitting on a chair.
c) They're making breakfast.

17. a) It isn't snowing. (It's not)
b) They aren't reading. (They're not)
c) She isn't swimming. (She's not)
d) He isn't sitting. (He's not)
e) I'm not leaving.
f) You aren't playing. (You're not)

18. a) We aren't singing. (We're not)
b) I'm not watching television.
c) She isn't running. (She's not)

Lösungen zu den Übungsaufgaben

19. a) Are you washing the window?
b) Am I looking in a mirror?
c) Is Mr Smith cooking dinner (lunch)?
d) Are Jenny and John reading books?
e) Is the girl playing football (with a ball)?
f) Are Mary and Jacky flying kites?
g) Is she riding a bike?

20. a) Is / buying / No, he isn't. (he's not)
b) Are / waiting / Yes, they are.
c) Is / riding / No, she isn't. (she's not)
d) Is / taking / Yes, he is.
e) Is the cat / Yes, it is.

21. a) Yes, he is.
b) No, they aren't. (they're not)
c) Yes, she is.
d) No, he isn't. (he's not)
e) No, it isn't. (it's not)

22. a) like / is raining
b) is staying / stays
c) is painting / reads
d) lives / is writing
e) visit / are watching
f) is / is getting
g) is barking / wants

23. a) comes
b) call
c) begins / snows
d) go
e) are trying
f) are having
g) are visiting / buy / go
h) likes / prefers
i) stays / goes.

24. a) lives
b) is repairing
c) Is / driving
d) Does / he doesn't
e) Are / playing / they are
f) doesn't live
g) are
h) Do / like / they do

Lösungen zu den Übungsaufgaben

i) Carol lives at 1, Wood Lane.
j) Karen lives at 2, Wood Lane.
k) Mandy and Ian live at 3, Wood Lane.
l) Mark lives at 4, Wood Lane.
m) Peter and Michelle live at 5, Wood Lane.
n) John lives at 6, Wood Lane.

25. close – closed
    paint – painted
    phone – phoned
    try – tried
    play – played
    repair – repaired
    dry – dried
    stop – stopped
    use – used

26. a) walked
    b) climbed
    c) opened
    d) used
    e) carried
    f) planned
    g) parked

27. a) Colin walked to work.
    b) Kim moved to a new house.
    c) Gill phoned her friend on Monday. (On Monday ...)
    d) Julie and Katie liked their holiday in Ireland.

28. a) He was in the kitchen.
    b) I was a teacher.
    c) She was outside the shop.
    d) They were on holiday.
    e) We were happy.
    f) You were in front of the post office.
    g) I was ready to go to school.
    h) She was with Jane.

Lösungen zu den Übungsaufgaben

29. a) Sally was in the garden.
b) Charles and Rebecca were good friends.
c) The car was green.

30. a) Geoff had sandwiches for his dinner.
b) Julie had a holiday in Ely.
c) I had cornflakes for breakfast.
d) Every day they had a walk in the park.
e) We had two pizzas in our car.

31. a) Linda had a horse.
b) Julie and Paul had a boat.
c) Wendy and Peter had an old car.
d) Mandy had a lot (lots) of books.

32. a) Lucy had an old magazine.
b) Yesterday, Arnold had his birthday. (... yesterday.)

33.

C	W	S	T	M	E		
A	E	A	H	A	W		
M	N	W	O	D	R		
E	T	P	U	E	O		
B	O	U	G	H	T		
G	O	T	H	M	E		
P	K	T	T	O	D		

bought   saw
came   took
got   thought
went   wrote
made
put

34.
a) went   b) went
c) took   d) bought
e) saw   f) took
g) made   h) thought / was
i) had   j) came (went)
k) wrote   l) had
m) put   n) was
o) went / bought   p) did

Lösungen zu den Übungsaufgaben

35.
a) took photos
b) sat
c) repaired
d) painted a picture (her house).
e) went to the bank.
f) washed her car.
g) played golf.

36.
a) We are going to fly to Paris.
b) We are going to stay in a hotel.
c) She is going to visit a museum.
d) He is going to write a lot of postcards. (lots of)
e) I'm going to paint a picture.
f) They are going to climb (go up) the Eiffel Tower.

37.
a) We're not going to use the car.
b) John isn't going to stay in bed.
c) Karen isn't going to go to the cinema.
d) Karen and John aren't going to watch television.
e) They aren't going to eat ice-cream.
f) I'm not going to buy chocolate.
g) I'm not going to wash up.

38.
a) I'm going to be beautiful.
b) He isn't going to swim here. (He's not)
c) We aren't going to run. (We're not)

39.
a) Is he going to ride his bicycle?
b) Are they going to drive their car?
c) Is she going to buy a camera?
d) Is it going to rain tomorrow?
e) Are we going to stay at John's house?
f) Are they going to sell their house?
g) Is she going to lock the door?
h) Is he going to clean the floor?

Lösungen zu den Übungsaufgaben

   i) Are they going to fly to Japan?
   j) Are we going to go skiing?
   k) Are you going to read a book?
   l) Is it going to work today?
   m) Is she going to eat the cake?

40. a) No, he isn't (he's not). He's going to paint it.
    b) No, they aren't (they're not). They're going to wash it.
    c) No, she isn't (she's not). She's going to buy a coat (jacket).
    d) No, it isn't (it's not). It's going to snow.
    e) No, we aren't (we're not). We're going to stay in (at) a hotel.
    f) No, they aren't (they're not). They're going to sell their motorbikes.

41. a) Are they going to stay here?
       No, they aren't (they're not). They're going to go to your hotel.
    b) Is she going to make breakfast?
       Yes, she is.
    c) Are you going to fetch (get) the ball?
       No, I'm not. I'm going to buy a new ball.
    d) Are you going to help her down?
       No, I'm not.
    e) Is he going to sit (sit down) here?
       Yes, he is, but ...

Hilfsverben

1. a) The bird is small. It is small.
      The bird is black. It's black.
   b) Carol is pretty. She is pretty.
      Carol is thin. She's thin.
   c) The house is new. It is new.
      The house is big. It's big.

Lösungen zu den Übungsaufgaben

d) Micky is a mouse. He is a mouse.
   Micky is white. He's white.
e) The flowers are beautiful. They are beautiful.
   The flowers are red. They're red.

2. a) I'm Gary.   b) We're UR11.
   c) Lucy is Scottish.   d) We're sisters.
   e) Colin is small (little).

3. a) isn't (is not / He's not)   b) aren't (are not / We're not)
   c) aren't (are not / They're not) d) 'm not (am not)
   e) aren't (are not / You're not) f) isn't (is not / She's not)

4. a) She isn't a footballer. (She's not)
      She's a horserider.
   b) He isn't a doctor. (He's not)
      He's a singer.
   c) They aren't dancers. (They're not)
      They're pilots.
   d) They aren't cooks. (They're not)
      They're footballers.

5. a) No, he isn't. (he's not)   b) Yes, she is.
   c) Yes, I am.   d) No, it isn't. (it's not)
   e) Yes, we are.

6. a) Are you in London?   No, I'm not.
   b) Is Julia a friend?   Yes, she is.
   c) Are they from Japan?   No, they're not.
   d) Am I the winner?   Yes, you are.
   e) Is Steve a policeman?   No, he isn't.

Lösungen zu den Übungsaufgaben

7. a) have got ice-creams. b) have got hats.
   c) has got a sandwich. d) have got umbrellas.
   e) has got a pair of gloves. f) has got a pair of sunglasses.

8. a) They've got hats and sunglasses.
   b) She's got a dog and a crocodile.
   c) He's got big feet.

9. a) I haven't got a dog. b) She hasn't got a camera.
   c) We haven't got pencils. d) They haven't got a car.

10. a) camel b) sea lion
   c) elephant d) boy
   e) girl f) monkey
   g) mouth h) hand
   i) eye j) nose
   k) leg l) ear

11. a) The camel hasn't got a mouth.
   b) They boy hasn't got a nose.
   c) The girl hasn't got a hand.
   d) The monkey hasn't got legs.
   e) The elephants haven't got ears.
   f) The sea lions haven't got eyes.

12. a) Has the house got a door?
   No, it hasn't.
   b) Have Mr and Mrs Smith got a dog?
   Yes, they have.
   c) Have the girls got long hair?
   Yes, they have.
   d) Has the girl got a book?
   No, she hasn't.

Lösungen zu den Übungsaufgaben

   e) Has the car got a radio?
      Yes, it has.
   f) Have John and Jenny got a boat?
      Yes, they have.
   g) Has Gordon got a train?
      No, he hasn't.
   h) Has the toy shop got a plant?
      No, it hasn't.
   i) Has Mary got a telephone?
      Yes, she has.
   j) Have the children got balls?
      Yes, they have.

13. a) 've got   b) Has it got
    c) hasn't   d) 've got
    e) Have you got   f) haven't

14. a) Julian can fly a plane. He can fly a plane.
    b) Mike and Sylvia can speak German. They can speak German.
    c) Amanda and Gary can play football. They can play football.
    d) Gary can play tennis. He can play tennis.
    e) Sylvia can make videos. She can make videos.

15. a) Mike, Amanda, Gary and Sylvia can't fly a plane.
    b) Julian, Amanda and Gary can't speak German.
    c) Julian, Sylvia and Mike can't play football.
    d) Julian, Sylvia, Mike and Amanda can't play tennis.
    e) Julian, Mike, Amanda and Gary can't make videos.

16. a) Can they ride bikes?
    b) Can they swim?
    c) Can Aunty Jane drive a car?
    d) Can you wash my car?
    e) Can Ann phone John?

Lösungen zu den Übungsaufgaben

    f) Can Peter and you play basketball?
    g) Can George make an English breakfast?
    h) Can Mary sing a song from Ireland?

17. a) No, they can't.   b) Yes, they can.
    c) Yes, she can.   d) No, I can't.
    e) Yes, she can.   f) No, we can't.
    g) No, he can't.   h) Yes, she can.

18. a) Martin and Kim may make breakfast.
    b) Jacky may close the window.
    c) Peter may go to the shop.
    d) Jenny may buy a new dress.
    e) Carol and Lucy may go to the pop concert.
    f) Ian may visit his friend.

19. a) May we open the packet of biscuits?
    b) May I have the ketchup?
    c) May Kim eat the sandwich?
    d) May Tim and Jenny have ice-creams? (an ice-cream)
    e) May Becky use the telephone?
    f) May Robert and I drink the lemonade?
    g) May I eat the apple?
    h) May we play games?

20. a) Can   b) May
    c) May   d) Can
    e) May   f) May / Can
    g) May   h) Can
    i) Can   j) May

21. a) Yes, he can.   b) No, you may not.
    c) No, you may not.   d) Yes, she can.

Lösungen zu den Übungsaufgaben

e) Yes, you may.
g) Yes, you may.
i) No, you can't.

f) No, you may not. / No, you can't.
h) Yes, I can.
j) No, she may not.

22. a) "I must make sandwiches."
    b) "I must find my umbrella."
    c) "We must buy a bottle of water."
    d) "You must bring me a map."
    e) "We must take our cameras."

23. a) You mustn't take photographs.
    b) She mustn't play football.
    c) They mustn't park (stop) here.
    d) He mustn't swim here.

24. a) Must we leave at 5.00 a.m.? b) Must I take my umbrella?
    c) Must Susie sit next to me?   d) Must we stay awake?
    e) Must dad drive (all the way)? f) Must you make sandwiches?

25. a) Yes, we must. (Yes, we have to.)
    b) No, you needn't.
    c) Yes, she must. (Yes, she has to.)
    d) No, you needn't.
    e) No, he needn't.
    f) No, I needn't.

26. a) Can   b) Can
    c) Must   d) Can
    e) Must   f) Can (Must)
    g) Must   h) Can
    i) Can

Lösungen zu den Übungsaufgaben

27.
- a) May
- b) Must
- c) Can
- d) Can
- e) Must
- f) Can
- g) May
- h) Can
- i) Can
- j) May / Must

28.
- a) Polly has got to meet her mother at 4.00 p.m.
- b) Polly has got to help her brother.
- c) Chris has got to clean his room.
- d) Chris and Polly haven't got to cross the main road.
- e) Polly has got to wake up early.
- f) Chris has got to write to Mr James.
- g) Chris and Polly haven't got to go skateboarding.
- h) Polly hasn't got to use the telephone.
- i) Chris and Polly haven't got to make a lot of noise.
- j) Chris has got to make breakfast.

29.
- a) Has Polly got to meet her mother at 4.00 p.m.?
- b) Has Polly got to help her brother?
- c) Has Chris got to clean his room?
- d) Have Chris and Polly got to cross the main road?
- e) Has Polly got to wake up early?
- f) Has Chris got to write to Mr James?
- g) Have Chris and Polly got to go skateboarding?
- h) Has Polly got to use the telephone?
- i) Have Chris and Polly got to make a lot of noise?
- j) Has Chris got to make breakfast?

30.
- a) I've got to read this book for school.
- b) They haven't got to fly to Belfast.
- c) Have we got to go by train?
- d) Have you got to write your postcards?

Lösungen zu den Übungsaufgaben

Gerundium

1. a) closing   b) hopping
   c) hoping   d) staying
   e) crying   f) lying
   g) cutting   h) standing
   i) going   j) running
   k) sitting   l) making
   m) playing   n) asking

2. a) Swimming   b) Dancing
   c) Climbing   d) Flying
   e) Skiing

3. a) Visiting New York   b) Cleaning windows
   c) Opening bottles   d) Tying shoelaces
   e) Phoning friends   f) Watching football
   g) Finding treasure   h) Buying socks

4. a) Writing books is difficult.   b) Jogging is fun.
   c) Playing basketball is Linda's hobby.

Imperativ

1. a) Kick it!   b) Climb over it!
   c) Look this way!   d) Go under it!
   e) Turn left!   f) Stop now!

2. a) Find it!   b) Kick it!
   c) Hold it!   d) Fetch it!
   e) Throw it!   f) Catch it!
   g) Clean it!   h) Knock at it!

i) Go out!
j) Open it!
k) Close it! (Shut it!)
l) Ring the bell!

3.
a) Don't stop (park) here.
b) Don't cycle on the motorway.
c) Don't swim here.
d) Don't play football in the park.
e) Don't feed the animals (in the zoo).
f) Don't climb the trees.
g) Don't drink the water.
h) Don't take photographs here.
i) Don't play loud music.
j) Don't walk on the grass.

4.
a) Don't paint the door green.
b) Don't go to the library.
c) Don't forget your umbrella.
d) Don't visit grandma.
e) Don't run to the bank.
f) Don't swim.
g) Don't climb that tree.

5.
a) Don't climb the trees!
b) Don't stand on the flowers !
c) Don't throw stones!
d) Don't fight!

Fragen mit Fragewörtern

1.
a) What is on the chair?
b) What have Lucy and Rebecca got in the box?
c) What has Ann got?
d) What are John and Mike doing?
e) What is the dog's name?
f) What are the cats doing?
g) What is on the table?
h) What is Tom carrying?

Lösungen zu den Übungsaufgaben

    i) What has John got?
    j) What is under the table?
    k) What is Rebecca wearing?

2. a) What have the dogs got?
    b) What is Jane carrying (wearing)?
    c) What has Tim got in his hand?

3. a) How much   b) How much
    c) How many   d) How
    e) How much   f) How many
    g) How much   h) How many

4. a) How old is Kathy?   b) How much lemonade has Henry got?

5. a) Where is / Your pen is on the floor.
    b) Where are / Your shoes are on the bed.
    c) Where is / Her coat is in the car.
    d) Where is / Mike is under a tree. (laying on the grass)
    e) Where are / They're on a bus.
    f) Where is / Bill is from America.
    g) Where in Great Britain are they from?
       They're from Scotland.
    h) Where is / The camera is in the cupboard.

6. a) Who is / Steve's friend is Sam.
    b) Who are / They're policemen.
    c) Who is / Mandy is playing football.
    d) Who is / Mrs Simpson is talking.
    e) Who are / Kim and Barry are visiting Aunty Jane.
    f) Who is / Lucy is in the café.
    g) Who is / Tina is phoning grandma.
    h) Who are / I'm meeting Ian.

Lösungen zu den Übungsaufgaben

7. a) Where b) What
   c) Who d) How many
   e) What f) Where
   g) Where h) Who
   i) How much j) What
   k) What l) How old
   m) Who n) Who
   o) How much p) Where

8. a) Who is in the garage? b) Where are the photographs?
   c) Who are George's friends? d) Where is Janice from?

9. a) Whose watch is this?
   b) Whose coats are those?
   c) Whose books are these?
   d) Whose pen is that?
   e) Whose gloves are those on the floor?
   f) Whose hat is that on the chair?

10. a) Who's b) Whose
    c) Whose d) Who's got
    e) Whose f) Who's
    g) Whose h) Who's got
    i) Who's j) Whose
    k) Who's

11. a) Who's got a new bicycle? b) Whose car is new?

12. a) (Textreihenfolge) What / How many / Where ... from / Where / Why / what
    b) hamburger(s)
    c) (Beispiele)
       he – her – hear – hello – handle – holiday – handball – hopscotch

Lösungen zu den Übungsaufgaben

a – am – arm – aunt – apple – across – address – alphabet – afternoon

me – met – made – model – minute – morning – milkman – magazine – marmalade

be – bed – bell – bread – banana – because – beautiful – basketball

up – use – unit – until – useful – usually – umbrella

red – read – ready – really – railway – remember

go – get – game – great – German – goodbye

ear – easy – early – enough – evening – exercise – expensive – everywhere

13.
- a) Why do
- b) When do
- c) Where do
- d) How much does
- e) What do
- f) How do
- g) What do
- h) Where does
- i) What does
- j) When do

14.
- a) Where does
- b) Why does (When does)
- c) Where does
- d) Why (How) does
- e) What do
- f) When does
- g) Why do
- h) How do
- i) When do
- j) Where does

15.
- a) Where does Tony buy his clothes?
- b) Why do you collect stamps?
- c) How does Karen go to school?

16.
- a) Who does Ann meet at the station?
- b) Who can Adam visit?
- c) Who must we telephone?
- d) Who do they talk to?
- e) Who can she play with?
- f) Who must Colin take to the party?

17. a) Who have I got to telephone? (Who must I telephone?)
    b) Who does she talk to?
    c) Who can she help?

18. (text order) How do / Why do / Who's got / Where's / Where's / Which / who's / Where're / How much / where can / Which (Whose) / Where're / Why do / What do

*there is-, there are-*Konstruktionen

1. a) There are two doctors.   b) There is an (one) apple.
   c) There are four houses.   d) There are six books.
   e) There is a (one) tree.   f) There is an (one) ice-cream.
   g) There are three cars.   h) There is a (one) bottle of water.

2. a) There is a bus stop in front of the clothes shop.
   b) There is a taxi in front of the post office.
   c) There is a bicycle in front of the bakery.
   d) There are two robbers in front of the bank.
   e) There is a policeman in front of the taxi.
   f) There is an old man in front of the shoe shop.
   g) There are four flowers in front of the window.
   h) There are two trees in front of the bank.
   i) There is a bus in front of the bookshop.

Lösungen zu den Übungsaufgaben

Homophone

1. (Textreihenfolge)
   a) it's / It's / Its
   b) it's / its
   c) It's / Its
   d) It's / Its / its / It's / it's / its
   e) It's / It's / it's / its / its / its / It's

2. a) Their
   b) There is
   c) There are / over there
   d) There (Over there)
   e) their
   f) there / there is
   g) their / over there
   h) their / Their / over there
   i) There are / their
   j) There are / there / their / there

3. a) your
   b) You're
   c) You're
   d) Your
   e) your / you're
   f) You're / your
   g) your
   h) your
   i) your / You're
   j) You're / your
   k) You're
   l) your
   m) Your / you're
   n) You're / your
   o) your
   p) your
   q) Your / your

4. a) Who's got
   b) Whose
   c) Who's
   d) Who's
   e) Whose
   f) Who's got
   g) Who's
   h) Whose
   i) Who's got
   j) Who's

247

Ihre Meinung ist uns wichtig!

Ihre Anregungen sind uns immer willkommen.
Bitte informieren Sie uns mit diesem Schein über Ihre Verbesserungsvorschläge!

Titel-Nr.	Seite	Fehler, Vorschlag

STARK
Damit lernen einfacher wird ... !

Bitte hier abtrennen

9-V1M

Bitte ausfüllen und im frankierten Umschlag an uns einsenden. Für Fensterkuverts geeignet.

**STARK Verlag
Postfach 1852
85318 Freising**

Zutreffendes bitte ankreuzen!

Die Absenderin/der Absender ist:

- ☐ Lehrer/in
- ☐ Fachbetreuer/in
  Fächer:
- ☐ Seminarlehrer/in
  Fächer:
- ☐ Regierungsfachberater/in
  Fächer:
- ☐ Oberstufenbetreuer/in
- ☐ Schulleiter/in
- ☐ Leiter/in Lehrerbibliothek
- ☐ Leiter/in Schülerbibliothek
- ☐ Referendar/in, Termin 2. Staatsexamen:
- ☐ Sekretariat
- ☐ Schüler/in, Klasse:
- ☐ Eltern
- ☐ Sonstiges:

Unterrichtsfächer: (Bei Lehrkräften!)

Kennen Sie Ihre Kundennummer?
Bitte hier eintragen.

Absender (Bitte in Druckbuchstaben!)

Name/Vorname

Straße/Nr.

PLZ/Ort

Telefon privat   Geburtsjahr

Schule/Schulstempel (Bitte immer angeben!)

Bitte hier abtrennen ✂

Sicher durch alle Klassen!

Theorie ist gut, Praxis ist besser. Deshalb enthalten unsere von Fachlehrern entwickelten Trainingsbände nicht nur alle nötigen Fakten, sondern jede Menge praxisgerechte Übungen mit vollständigen Lösungen. Auf die prüfungsrelevanten Stoffgebiete konzentriert, ermöglichen alle Bände ein effektives Lernen – beste Voraussetzungen, um sicher durch alle Prüfungen zu kommen.

Mathematik

Zentrale Klassenarbeit Mathematik
Aufgaben zur Vorbereitung auf den Unterricht der 10. Klasse und die zentrale Klassenarbeit an baden-württembergischen Gymnasien. Mit Lösungen.
■ Best.-Nr. 80001 .... DM 17,90

Algebra 10. Klasse
Potenzen mit natürlichen Zahlen als Exponenten, Potenzen mit ganzzahligen Exponenten, Potenzen mit reellen Exponenten; Potenzfunktionen; Exponential- und Logarithmusfunktionen.
■ Best.-Nr. 90014 .... DM 19,90

Geometrie 10. Klasse – 1
Raumgeometrie: Zylinder, Kegel, Kugel; Ebene Geometrie: Kreismessung.
■ Best.-Nr. 90024 .... DM 17,90

Geometrie 10. Klasse – 2
Winkelfunktionen im rechtwinkligen Dreieck, Berechnung allg. Dreiecke, trigonometrische Funktionen und ihre Graphen, Additionstheoreme.
■ Best.-Nr. 90025 .... DM 17,90

Algebra 9. Klasse
Quadratwurzeln, quadratische Gleichungen, Bruch- und Wurzelgleichungen, quadratische Funktionen, Aufstellen von Parabelgleichungen etc.
■ Best.-Nr. 90013 .... DM 20,90

Geometrie 9. Klasse
Zentrische Streckung und Ähnlichkeit, Strahlensatz, Satzgruppe des Pythagoras, Pyramide.
■ Best.-Nr. 90023 .... DM 19,90

Algebra 8. Klasse
Bruchterme, Gleichungen und Ungleichungen, lineare Funktionen und Gleichungssysteme.
■ Best.-Nr. 90012 .... DM 18,90

Geometrie 8. Klasse
Vierecke, Kreis und Gerade, Flächenmessung, Einführung in die Raumgeometrie. Dazu Wiederholung wichtiger Inhalte der Geometrie 7. Klasse.
■ Best.-Nr. 90022 .... DM 19,90

Algebra 7. Klasse
Rationale Zahlen, Termumformungen, lineare Gleichungen und Ungleichungen, Textaufgaben.
■ Best.-Nr. 90011 .... DM 17,90

Geometrie 7. Klasse
Grundbegriffe der ebenen Geometrie, geometrisches Zeichnen; Winkel; Symmetrie und Kongruenz geometrischer Figuren; Dreiecke.
■ Best.-Nr. 90021 .... DM 17,90

Mathematik 6. Klasse
Rechnen mit Bruchzahlen, Dezimalbrüche, Prozentrechnung, geometrische Grundbegriffe, Proportionalität.
■ Best.-Nr. 90006 .... DM 19,90

Mathematik Bruchzahlen und Dezimalbrüche NEU
Grundrechenarten mit Bruchzahlen und Dezimalbrüchen, Vergleichen und Ordnen, Verbindung der Grundrechenarten, Umwandeln von Bruchzahlen und umgekehrt, Gleichungen/Ungleichungen etc.
■ Best.-Nr. 900061 .... DM 18,90

Mathematik 5. Klasse
Die vier Grundrechenarten, natürliche Zahlen, Größen und Sachaufgaben, geometrische Grundbegriffe, Teilbarkeit natürlicher Zahlen.
■ Best.-Nr. 90005 .... DM 19,90

Mathematik – Übertritt ins Gymnasium
Aufbau des Zahlensystems, die vier Grundrechenarten, Maße, Textaufgaben, Prüfungsaufgaben.
■ Best.-Nr. 90001 .... DM 17,90

Ratgeber für Schüler

Richtig Lernen
Tipps und Lernstrategien
für die 5. bis 7. Klasse – mit Elternbegleitheft
■ Best.-Nr. 10481 .... DM 12,90

(Bitte blättern Sie um)

Deutsch

Zentrale Klassenarbeit Deutsch **NEU**
Aufgaben zur Vorbereitung auf den Unterricht der 10. Klasse und die zentrale Klassenarbeit an baden-württembergischen Gymnasien. Mit Lösungen.
- Best.-Nr. 80402 .... DM 17,90

Deutsch – Aufsatz 9./10. Klasse
Beispiele und Übungsaufgaben mit Lösungen.
- Best.-Nr. 90404 .... DM 19,90

Deutsch – Grammatik 7./8. Klasse **NEU**
Beispiele und Übungsaufgaben mit Lösungen.
- Best.-Nr. 90407 .... DM 19,90

Deutsch – Aufsatz 7./8. Klasse
Beispiele und Übungsaufgaben mit Lösungen.
- Best.-Nr. 90403 .... DM 18,90

Deutsch – Grammatik 5./6. Klasse **NEU**
Beispiele und Übungsaufgaben mit Lösungen.
- Best.-Nr. 90406 .... DM 19,90

Deutsch – Aufsatz 5./6. Klasse
Beispiele und Übungsaufgaben mit Lösungen.
- Best.-Nr. 90401 .... DM 18,90

Deutsche Rechtschreibung 5.–10. Klasse
Beispiele und Übungsaufgaben mit Lösungen.
- Best.-Nr. 93442 .... DM 16,90

Englisch

Englisch – Übertritt in die Oberstufe
Wortschatz, Grammatik und Textproduktion werden anhand von Aufgaben mit Lösungen trainiert.
- Best.-Nr. 82453 .... DM 20,90

Englisch – Wortschatzübung Mittelstufe **NEU**
Abwechslungsreiche Übungen und Lösungen. Mit dazugehörigen Wortschatzlisten und Idioms.
- Best.-Nr. 90520 .... DM 19,90

Englisch 10. Klasse
Beispiele und Übungsaufgaben mit Lösungen.
- Best.-Nr. 90510 .... DM 18,90

Englisch – Hörverstehen 10. Klasse
Texte, von native speakers gesprochen, mit Aufgaben und Lösungen. **CD mit Begleitbuch.**
- Best.-Nr. 80457 .... DM 24,90

Zentrale Klassenarbeit Speziell für Baden-Württemberg
Texte, von native speakers gesprochen, mit Aufgaben und Lösungen. **CD mit Begleitbuch.** Inhaltlich identisch mit Best.-Nr. 80457.
- Best.-Nr. 80456 .... DM 24,90

Comprehension 3 / 10. Klasse
Beispiele und Übungsaufgaben mit Lösungen.
- Best.-Nr. 91454 .... DM 16,90

Translation Practice 2 / ab 10. Klasse
Beispiele und Übungsaufgaben mit Lösungen.
- Best.-Nr. 80452 .... DM 15,90

Englisch – Leseverstehen 10. Klasse **NEU**
Texte und Fragen mit Lösungen.
- Best.-Nr. 90521 .... DM 18,90

Englische Rechtschreibung – 9./10. Klasse
Beispiele und Übungsaufgaben mit Lösungen.
- Best.-Nr. 80453 .... DM 15,90

Englisch 9. Klasse
Beispiele und Übungsaufgaben mit Lösungen.
- Best.-Nr. 90509 .... DM 18,90

Translation Practice 1 / ab 9. Klasse
Beispiele und Übungsaufgaben mit Lösungen.
- Best.-Nr. 80451 .... DM 15,90

Comprehension 2 / 9. Klasse
Beispiele und Übungsaufgaben mit Lösungen.
- Best.-Nr. 91452 .... DM 14,90

Englisch – Hörverstehen 9. Klasse **NEU**
Texte, von native speakers gesprochen, mit Aufgaben und Lösungen. **CD mit Begleitbuch.**
- Best.-Nr. 90515 .... DM 24,90

Englisch 8. Klasse
Beispiele und Übungsaufgaben mit Lösungen.
- Best.-Nr. 90508 .... DM 18,90

Comprehension 1 / 8. Klasse
Beispiele und Übungsaufgaben mit Lösungen.
- Best.-Nr. 91453 .... DM 14,90

Englisch 7. Klasse **NEU**
Beispiele und Übungsaufgaben mit Lösungen.
- Best.-Nr. 90507 .... DM 18,90

Englisch 6. Klasse
Beispiele und Übungsaufgaben mit Lösungen.
- Best.-Nr. 90506 .... DM 18,90

Englisch – Hörverstehen 6. Klasse
Texte, von native speakers gesprochen, mit Aufgaben und Lösungen. **CD mit Begleitbuch.**
- Best.-Nr. 90511 .... DM 24,90

Englisch 5. Klasse
Beispiele und Übungsaufgaben mit Lösungen.
- Best.-Nr. 90505 .... DM 18,90

Englisch – Hörverstehen 5. Klasse
Texte, von native speakers gesprochen, mit Aufgaben und Lösungen. **CD mit Begleitbuch.**
- Best.-Nr. 90512 .... DM 24,90

Englisch – Rechtschreibung und Diktat 5. Klasse **NEU**
Texte und Übungen, von native speakers gesprochen, mit Lösungen. **CD mit Begleitbuch.**
- Best.-Nr. 90531 .... DM 24,90

Bestellungen bitte direkt an: Stark Verlag · Postfach 1852 · 85318 Freising
Tel. 0 81 61/17 90 · FAX 0 81 61/179 51 · Internet http://www.stark-verlag.de
Unverbindliche Preisempfehlung.

STARK
Damit lernen einfacher wird ... !